STILL
RANTING

STILL RANTING

MORE RANTS, RAVES AND RECOLLECTIONS

RAFE MAIR

whitecap

*To Wendy, the love of my life, who is, in no particular order, my
fishing buddy, my pal, my lover and my web mistress—and the
one who keeps me from getting into even more trouble.*

Copyright © 2002 by Rafe Mair
Whitecap Books

The opinions in this book in no way represent the views of Whitecap Books Ltd.

Edited by Ann-Marie Metten
Proofread by Elizabeth Salomons
Book design by Roberta Batchelor
Type layout by Jane Lightle
Cover photographs by Ryan McNair
Illustrations: FotoSearch (www.fotosearch.com)

Printed and bound in Canada

National Library of Canada Cataloguing in Publication Data

Mair, Rafe, 1931–
  Still ranting: more rants, raves and recollections

  ISBN 1-55285-401-9

  I. Title.
AC8.M315 2002   081   C2002-910886-1

The publisher acknowledges the support of the Canada Council for the Arts and the
Cultural Services Branch of the Government of British Columbia for our publishing pro-
gram. We acknowledge the financial support of the Government of Canada through the
Book Publishing Industry Development Program for our publishing activities.

At Whitecap Books we are committed to protecting the environment and to the
responsible use of natural resources. We are acting on this commitment by working
with suppliers and printers to phase out our use of paper produced from ancient
forests. This book is printed by Friesens on 100% post-consumer recycled paper,
processed chlorine free and printed with vegetable based inks. We are working with
Markets Initiative (www.oldgrowthfree.com) on this project.

CONTENTS

ON POLITICS

DRIFTING LEFT

One is supposed to become large "C" conservative as one gets older. Radical politician and journalist Georges Clemenceau, when he learned that his son was a communist, is reputed to have said, "If he had not become a Communist at twenty-two, I would have disowned him. If he is still a Communist at thirty, I will do it then." I find myself, at seventy, paddling furiously against the current. I may be getting more conservative all right, but definitely with a small "c" and definitely not on social or fiscal issues. I believe that to be conservative means to protect what we have, especially in the environment. I am, in short, an environmentalist.

The term "conservative" has been turned on its head over the last fifty years. Conservatives are seen today to be people such as former President Ronald Reagan, who made the rapacious James Watt his secretary of the interior and instructed him to give away to land developers that which they had not already stolen. The federal Liberals in Canada are no better. One only has to look at the politicization of the Department of Fisheries and Oceans under their watch. Protection of ocean resources has come to mean dividing them among wealthy scum who haven't the faintest concern for the blessings of nature that God bestowed on us. In fairness to the federal Liberals—and it is difficult to do that—the process of failing to conserve our natural resources was started by the Mulroney Conservatives and his ministerial suck Tom Siddon. In 1984 he would cheerfully have sacrificed two major sockeye runs to let Alcan totally bugger up the Nechako River with the Kemano Completion Project. It is to Premier

Mike Harcourt of the NDP that credit must be given for stopping this monumental rape of our environment and natural resources.

Left and right have each contributed to a blurring of the environmental issues. We have created a left that is supposed to love the environment and hate business and a right that hates, or at best is indifferent to, the environment and loves big business. These definitions have become self-fulfilling prophecies as right-wing governments always put jobs far ahead of the environment and long-term considerations. Meanwhile left-wing governments do precisely the same thing but protest all the while.

Big business wants lots of oil extraction, felling of trees, ill-controlled pulp mills and huge power projects. But so do the labour unions, and with gusto. This explains what to the left-wing, such as the NDP, has always been the unexplainable— why their members submit to having their dues paid to the NDP while they themselves vote for right-wing parties.

Big business always pays lip service to helping those who need help while doing all it can to prevent help from happening. The left jumps into the "poor" game with great gusto and usually does a worse job for the underprivileged than does the right, if only because the right brings to the task an element of competence. (Those who, in the bad old Socred days, pilloried then Welfare Minister Grace McCarthy will, to a person, concede that she was a far better minister than anyone the left ever threw into the exercise.)

It is in the hands of big business that we place the health of the environment, our own personal health and our very lives. For example, most people think that products from drug companies are released for sale in Canada only after the government has carefully tested them. Well, that's not true. All the tests are done by company scientists whose work is then, often scantily, examined by government scientists. Tests do not follow the proper scientific method, which requires a healthy skepticism at every turn, a constant surveillance by the "devil's advocate," so to speak. Science has not only invented but marketed disastrous innovations such as DDT, thalidomide, IUD birth control and faulty breast implants. They did so with the assurance that they were fine for common use. It took courageous individuals such as Rachel Carson with her blockbuster exposé of DDT in *Silent Spring* (Houghton Mifflin, 1962) and the courage of the London *Sunday Times* to flush out the truth about thalidomide in the 1970s. Governments were no help. It is now becoming more clear every day that aspartame, commonly known as NutraSweet, is little short of poisonous. Further, health authorities have warned that eating more than one farmed salmon a week is dangerous. The plain fact is that neither the companies nor the government do the important part of testing. They leave it to the public. We are guinea pigs for the world of science. We trust big business when they tell us about genetically modified foods, including genetically modified, insect-resistant grain. We accept the word of any man in a white coat who points at a blackboard covered with scientific hieroglyphics.

We are in the hands of what has now become a virtually unrestricted international business cartel, where even the environmental and social decisions are made in boardrooms far from the prying eyes of governments, who are eunuchs in the industrial harem.

The left argues that we abandoned our sovereignty with the Canada–U.S. Free Trade Agreement and NAFTA, whereas in fact these agreements only put in writing what the computer had already made a reality. It was the silicon chip that took away from government the power to control money. When George Soros, a money gambler, beat out the U.K. government for a cool billion in the exchange rate mechanism debacle of the Major government in 1993, it told all. Countries no longer controlled their currency. That was the loss of sovereignty, not NAFTA.

The struggle for the environment and against conservatism has been a terrible one for me. I am a capitalist by instinct and I reject the notion of planned economies and socialism. Yet I am an environmentalist with the credentials to prove it. In the spring of 1979, as B.C. Minister of Environment, I took the side of the environmentalists and helped save the Skagit River from destruction by the Americans, who were raising the Ross Dam as they were entitled to under an ancient agreement with the B.C. government. I fought the Kemano Completion Project in 1994 and that year received the Michener Award for Journalism for my efforts. I helped save the Upper Pitt River from desecration by a gravel pit in 2000. Few have fought the Atlantic salmon fish farmers with more ferocity than have I. I am no "condominium conservationist." I bear the scars from battles to preserve our heritage.

Yet I believe that competition is bred into our beings and that our society, if it is to survive and prosper, must be a meritocracy. I hate incompetence, something that parties of the left seem to have in enormous abundance. I believe that the marketplace and its forces must be understood and obeyed in an ameliorated way in a caring society.

And perhaps that's where I'm coming from. I care and I want a society that cares.

Let me sum up my feelings with a generalization. Those of the "right," even (perhaps especially) those capitalists who once suffered privation, invariably say that they believe in support for the poor. But they see welfare fraud behind every potted palm in their private clubs, where they rip off the tax system by charging each others' whiskeys and canapés against their personal taxes. The right can't wait for the anecdotal evidence (which can always be found) of "welfare Wednesday," when tens of thousands take taxis to the welfare office to pick up their cheques on their way to the local pub. The right lap up stories of single mothers who borrow from the government to go back to school to earn a BA, and thus join a more elegant unemployment line. They would have saved society the money if they'd only got a decent job (which wasn't there in the first place, that being the whole point).

The right pretend that they are not homophobic yet it seems that every time the leader of the Alliance Party underscores that point, one of their MPs makes a gutter remark confirming suspicions.

The right pretend not to be racist but most usually are; not all are racist of course, but always enough to enforce the argument.

Corporations don't give a damn about the environment except to the extent that governments force them to care. The right sees the achievements of Greenpeace and of my personal hero, Paul Watson of the Sea Shepherd Society, and calls them excesses. They don't see the ruined fish habitat, plundered oceans, dead sea birds in drift nets, decimated species nor do they care to see them. I recall an on-air argument with a member of the Fraser Institute, which continued when its director, Dr. Michael Walker, phoned me at home. The Fraser Institute's position was that rivers should be privately owned because private ownership would put them to their best available economic use that, according to their argument, would be to preserve salmon for fishing. Yeah, sure. Just as happened to the Rhine, the Thames and to every other river that industry came near and saw as a wonderful, natural sewer.

What must be accepted as axiomatic is that capital, like a stiff cock, has no conscience. None. It is in the interests of capital to make as much return as possible from as little expenditure as possible. To pretend otherwise is calamitous self-delusion. Yet we pretend otherwise and so do the governments we elect. Politicians will readily tell you that capital provides jobs, which it does. But it does so as a necessary nuisance. If General Motors could manufacture and sell its cars using nothing but robots, then they would, without the slightest hesitation. If not forced otherwise by union contracts, they would lay off every employee in the blink of an eyelash. If pulp companies could dump all their industrial waste into the nearest river or ocean they would do so without hesitation. Moreover, as we saw in the Westray mining disaster in Nova Scotia in 1992, capital cares little if at all about the safety of its workers. Without government regulations, workers' compensation and trade unions, there would be very little in the way of concern for workers' safety.

I do not say these things with a sneer on my face indicating some inherent dislike of industry, of capitalism or of the free market system. Not at all. For if we want to see the very worst in environmental ravages and contempt for worker safety, we need only look at the workers' "paradises" that existed before the Iron Curtain fell in 1989. The ravages of the "peoples'" democracies are felt to this day.

No, my point is simple. We must recognize the aim of capital and protect ourselves accordingly. We must never accept the word of capital that what they are about to do is in the general public good. Although it may be true, it must be accepted as true only after it has been tested severely.

And here's the rub. Far too often the onus is on a caring public to demonstrate that a project is unsafe instead of the other way around. As an example, look at the current dispute around Atlantic salmon fish farms on the B.C. coast. Why should the onus be on the public to demonstrate that escaped Atlantics will spawn in our rivers and take them over from Pacific salmon? Why should the David Suzuki Foundation, the T. Buck Suzuki Environmental Foundation (no relation), the Steelhead Society of British Columbia, native groups and sports anglers to name but a few interested groups—plus, of course, the general public—have to demonstrate the dangers of disease from fish farms and the dangers from their sewage and the sea lice they place in the paths of juvenile wild salmon on their way to sea? These are matters of deep public concern. Why isn't a public regulator, the government, in place with rules to enforce? Why doesn't the industry have to prove beyond a reasonable doubt that what they will do will be done safely?

The answer is tragic. Under so-called "right-wing" governments the policing agencies of governments have been castrated. The federal Department of Fisheries is now an industrial development arm of government with the mandate to develop aquaculture, which is to say fish farming.

Do these complaints make me a socialist? Certainly not. Governments make lousy business people. Whenever they get into business they make a hash of it. When they try to encourage certain businesses through tax breaks or outright grants they invariably get it wrong. And it's not only left-wing governments that screw up. All governments do best when they stay the hell away from the marketplace, except as regulators and as police in other areas where order and safety are required.

I shudder when I hear the cry to get rid of "red tape." Not that we shouldn't constantly try to keep regulations comprehensible, meaningful and enforced in a timely manner, but I hear this complaint often as code words for the principle that we "let industry decide what is best for society."

I part from the left in that I know they are so inefficient as to become hugely expensive to the point of fiscal ruin. I part from the right on their contention that development is good by definition and that we must always have "progress."

I believe our society must severely examine its game plan. What is it we want? Do we care about social values? Are we prepared to have less "progress" and a more wholesome environment?

Let me tell you my values. I will not likely ever see a penguin in Antarctica yet I would be deeply concerned if, because big business has exploited their krill, the penguin suffered unto extinction. I never see the whales Paul Watson saves yet I support his work in every way I can. I have never seen a kiwi in the wild but would feel a deep pain if it became extinct. I have not seen a grizzly bear in fifty years but I want to know they are there.

We are forever being told that we must compete for industry with Alberta and that we must therefore be "friendlier" to the capital that wishes to invest in our province. But does "friendlier" have to mean that we allow capital and industry to do what they wish with us? Isn't the fact that employees will work in British Columbia and not in Alberta a friendly gesture and a selling point, if it is properly made in a timely fashion? Even if we can't and don't compete, is that the end of the world? If we make less money, and if people like me who make plenty of money have to pay a bit more in taxes, is that so bad if we have our fish still with us, our grizzlies safe from the guns of wealthy Germans and a few more views uncontaminated by clear cuts?

Must we have more and more people? Doesn't there logically have to come a time when we have far too many? And when that day comes won't we be forced to do what China is doing, namely develop an economy that is utterly free from all environmental constraints?

Don't we then have to accept the unacceptable? And, even if we, in our limited lifespans avoid the worst of all this, is this what we wish as our legacy to generations yet to come?

More and more, in my closing years, I find myself identifying with the words of John Donne's *Devotions Upon Emergent Occasions* (1623):

> No man is an Iland, intire of it selfe; every man is a peece of the Continent, a part of the maine; if a Clod bee washed away by the Sea, Europe is the lesse, as well as if a Promontorie were, as well as if a Mannor of thy friends, or of thine owne were; Any mans death diminishes me, because I am involved in Mankinde; And therefore never send to know for whom the bell tolls; It tolls for thee.

Sad to say, perhaps the good doctor had the tense wrong. Perhaps the bell has already tolled.

IN CANADA THE SKIM RISES

The terrible events of September 11, 2001, allowed Canadians to watch American politicians deal honourably with the New York tragedy and compare them with our own bumbling politicians. It wasn't a pretty sight.

First, Prime Minister Chrétien, after a high on September 14 when he addressed the crowd in Ottawa on the day of national mourning, quickly took on his more accustomed role of parish-pump politician. He couldn't get himself to "ground zero," the site of the World Trade Center rubble, for another two weeks. President Jacques Chirac of France made it. Britain's Prime Minister Blair made it, and who will forget the camera focussed on Mr. Blair during President Bush's address to Congress on November 20? Where was Mr. Chrétien? And why did President Bush deliberately omit the word "Canada" from his unforgettable and most Churchillian speech that evening?

Within a few weeks of the 9-11 catastrophe, we watched Immigration Minister Elinor Caplan trip all over her tongue as she tried to come to grips with our immigration and refugee problem, let alone deal with the notion of a one border policy for all of North America. Canadians witnessed the spectacle of Hedy Fry, surely the worst cabinet minister on earth, utterly at sea at the conference on racism in Durban, South Africa (which was really a talk shop for anti-Israeli propaganda). Ms. Fry, later and belatedly sacked, then followed this outrage by continuing to sit on a public platform while University of British Columbia professor Sunera Thobani, to the horror of most Canadians, told how the United States had got what it deserved.

Then Transport Minister David Collenette demonstrated, as if that were needed, his utter lack of competence as he tried to deal with flights diverted from La Guardia Airport and restrictions on international and trans-border flights. Following that, Collenette announced compensation for losses Air Canada experienced because of the closure of Canada's airspace following September 11. In reality most of these problems related not to the events of September 11 as Air Canada claimed, but to Mr. Collenette's bungling of the Air Canada–Canadian Airlines merger the summer before. Even Foreign Minister John Manley, usually sure-footed, babbled all over the place on my radio show as he avoided all direct questions about Canada's weird response to the New York tragedy. He simply parroted the usual pre-programmed answers for which federal Liberal cabinet ministers are famous.

Contrast these embarrassments if you will with those of three American politicians in the days following September 11. Democratic Senator Tom Daschle, majority leader in the Senate, and Republican Senator Trent Lott, minority leader, on September 20, the night the president addressed a joint meeting of Congress, offered bipartisan support. Their effort was significant in that these bright, independent politicians didn't support President Bush because they had to out of any political loyalty, but because they had done their homework. They supported Bush because they were convinced he was doing the right thing for America. They held up no caveats that would have permitted them to withdraw support if things didn't go as planned. Instead, here were two leaders who knew their duty and were competent enough to articulate it in plain, unadorned English.

House Leader Richard Gephardt, the man who will, I predict, be the next banner carrier for the Democrats, spent many hours under intense media scrutiny and looked every inch the statesman. The reason that he and other American politicians such as Secretary of State Colin Powell and Secretary of Defense Donald Rumsfeld looked so superior to anyone we could cough up here in Canada is that, in fact, they are superior. Under the American system the president can look to the entire nation when selecting a cabinet. Cabinet officers by law may not be members of Congress. I certainly don't say that all American senators and representatives are superior to all Canadian counterparts—just that most of them are. And the reason for the difference is the systems under which they operate.

A member of the House of Representatives or the U.S. Senate must show merit or he or she doesn't get elected. In each case the job requires individual thinking. I'm not by any means saying that there are not political realities facing the member of the U.S. Congress—there are many. But because the government cannot be brought down by an adverse vote in either American house, the member has much more independence. He or she is not subject to orders from the president nor can the president keep him or her from running on the party ticket. That's of course the Canadian leader's nuclear weapon. For these reasons, members of Congress and the Senate are likely to be made of pretty stern stuff. And because of their political system, the American voter is not impressed by the party hack but insists on electing someone who knows his or her own mind.

The Canadian politician, on the other hand, must, if he or she is to be successful, be a toady. That's a condition precedent. In order to get ahead he or she must do as told. Instructions come from the prime minister's office through the party whip. Any effort at individual thought by an MP is discouraged; any attempt at individual action is stamped out immediately.

Many parts of the American system are unsavoury, the principal one being the amount of money it costs to get elected. That, however, is a functional problem, not a systemic one. It is an abuse Congress has the power to end. Any reasonable view of American representatives and senators, especially after such significant events as September 11, demonstrates that the American political product is vastly superior to the supine lickspittles produced on this side of the border. Whenever they open their mouths, the proof is obvious.

WHO NEEDS HEROES?

The death on December 6, 2001, of New Zealand yachtsman Sir Peter Blake at the hands of pirates in the Brazilian Amazon put the worldwide yachting community into mourning. It also plunged the entire nation of New Zealand into deep grief—New Zealand Parliament was briefly suspended and flags were flown at half-mast—as the entire country mourned the loss of the man who took the 1995 America's Cup from San Diego to Auckland. It was only the second time in the event's 144-year history that a non-American team had won the coveted silver trophy. To top it off, Blake kept the cup in New Zealand following the 2000 race, as well. When he was killed, there was little talk of anything else on the talk shows, in the bars and restaurants and in the street.

New Zealand, a country you could put many times inside British Columbia but which has the same population, has had many national heroes. Peter Snell, the great runner and gold medal winning runner at the 1960 and 1964 Olympics, Sir Richard Hadlee the world record holder in cricket, and Sir Edmund Hillary, the conqueror of Mount Everest, are but three of New Zealand's heroes in the modern era. The tragic death of any of them in their prime would have brought, I daresay, the same sort of national grief brought on by the death of Sir Peter Blake.

You sense the question, don't you? Name a Canadian alive today who would merit this reaction from Canadians. One.

Wayne Gretzky in his prime? Maybe, though I doubt it. Oh, there would have been sorrow—deep sorrow—and hockey rinks across the country would have been draped in black crepe. CBC would have broadcast his funeral. But not even Wayne Gretzky could have united Canada the way Blake united New Zealand. Whatever his enormous talents and whatever his contribution to Canada's pathetic standing on the world stage of sport, even in his prime Wayne Gretzky fell far short of the stature in his country of Sir Peter Blake.

Terry Fox? Perhaps Terry is the closest Canada has ever come to celebrating a hero. While his death did bring great grief, I think it fell short of uniting the nation.

Pierre Trudeau? Not a chance. His death, while it created a great spectacle, was just that, a spectacle that reflected the ongoing curiosity Canadians maintain for a man half the nation detested. Trudeau's death provided the CBC a great opportunity to trot out all their old tape, but were there huge outbursts of public mourning across the country? Were there memorial services in every hamlet? Scarcely, and though it's hard to spit it out it must be said that, had Trudeau died in office, Alberta at least would have celebrated and perhaps British Columbia would have, too. How about Brian Mulroney? I only include his name to give you a good belly laugh. Any of the present lot of politicians? Ha! There's more feeling in Canada for Israel Mora, the Mexican performance artist who obtained public funds, both Mexican and Canadian, for jacking off into vials and displaying them as art, in seriousness—a seriousness shared by the government—at the Banff Centre in December 2001. There's more feeling for this so-called artist than there is for the likes of Jean Chrétien, Alexa McDonough or Stephen Harper. No, I challenge you all. Name one Canadian whose untimely death would send this nation into national grief.

There isn't one.

What does this tell us?

I think it tells us that we utterly refuse to accept heroes. I don't think there's anything we can do about it or anything we should. Most Canadians, as it is, cringe at the breast-beating ads the

Canadian government flogs. Canadians didn't know whether to laugh or cry back in 1996 when Heritage Minister Sheila Copps dished out $25 million for the distribution of a million free Canadian flags for National Flag Day on February 15, 1997. Interestingly, Doreen Braverman, a former B.C. Liberal leader and owner of The Flag Shop in Vancouver, was outraged at the unfair competition.

We are skeptical of heroes and our patriotism lies more in a hatred of national institutions, such as, in its time, the CPR, and always the CBC and Air Canada; a detestation of all that Toronto stands for; feeling generally pissed off with Quebec; and a fear of absorption by the United States (a diminishing fear, I might add).

Let me put to you the final patriotic test. If a foreign country were to invade the outermost rock of Great Britain or if the Russians sent so much as a squad of soldiers to some hitherto unknown piece of desolate granite in the Aleutians, there would be all hell to pay. But what if the Americans were to invade Newfoundland? Would you send your sons and daughters to war? What if they invaded Toronto (no fair cheering here) or even Vancouver?

After losing such a war, would British Columbians take to the hills in guerrilla warfare as have the Chechnyans?

An honest answer would be that life would go on. The American dollar would be in circulation, the anthem would change and the place we hate most would be Washington, D.C., instead of Ottawa. And we'd be rid of the bloody Liberals forever.

Canadians, emotionally, are dead from the ass up and that's the truth of the matter.

Period.

THE UNKNOWN CANADIAN

Canadians are famous for refusing to countenance heroes. We've had plenty of heroes, of course, but we prefer to knock them down before they even have a chance to mount a pedestal.

How many of us know that a Canadian was once prime minister of Great Britain? Andrew Bonar Law, a man born and raised in Kingston, County of Kent, Province of New Brunswick, moved to Scotland at age sixteen to study at the University of Glasgow and then to work for his family's firm of merchant bankers. Law was Britain's premier for less than two years in 1922–23, but he was no John Turner or Kim Campbell for he won, in 1922, a watershed victory for the Tories. It was death, not defeat that took Bonar Law out of politics.

The Conservatives had been in the wilderness after Balfour lost in 1906. Worse than that, the charismatic Liberal government of David Lloyd George had been in power during the final and decisive years of the First World War. But Bonar Law's win in 1922 brought the Tories back into power.

When the Liberals took office in 1906, and especially after Herbert Asquith took over in 1908, they were determined to reform and reform they did. With the likes of Lloyd George and Churchill directing social reform and with a party bent on reducing to nothing the powers of the House of Lords, the Liberals looked as if they had become the natural governing party they'd been in Gladstone's day.

In the middle of the First World War, the Liberals sagged and, under enormous pressure from the Conservative and Labour parties, changed leadership from Asquith to Lloyd George, who formed a coalition government. Bonar Law, the leader of the Tories after Balfour resigned in 1911, became deputy prime minister and chancellor of the exchequer responsible for financing the war effort. He was, in effect, Lloyd George's partner for the remaining three years of the war. After the war, the coalition won what was known as the coupon election because the coalition gave Tories and Liberals who were loyal to the coalition a "coupon" to so indicate to the electors—which for the first time included women over thirty, incidentally—that they were endorsed by the coalition. It was clear that the coalition had in fact come apart if only because the Liberal Party remained badly split between the Asquith Liberals and the Lloyd George Liberals. In a famous meeting at the Carleton Club, the Tory London club, in October 1922, the Conservatives voted to dissolve the coalition. In short order Bonar Law was prime minister. A few months later he called an election, won a resounding victory and brought a young man name Stanley Baldwin into cabinet.

Baldwin would succeed him a few months later to the surprise and dismay of George, Lord Curzon, the aristocracy's aristocrat, who thought he had a lock on the job and didn't need to stoop to politics to get it. He was wrong. With the exception of two minority Labour governments, which held power only at the sufferance of the Tories, the Conservatives remained in power until 1945.

When Bonar Law died of throat cancer in 1923 he was given a state funeral and buried in Westminster Abbey, prompting a wag to observe how fitting it was that the Unknown prime minister was buried next to the Unknown Soldier.

Bonar Law may have been prime minister for only a few months but his services were great indeed. The electoral successes of the Conservative Party until a couple of years ago were in large measure the result of Law's virtual banishing of the Liberal Party to permanent rump status. Law left opposition to the Labour Party, who the public had not seen as a real alternative until after the war in 1945.

The efforts of Law had another consequence, perhaps unintended. The Liberal Party never recovered. The split Lloyd George caused when he knocked over Asquith in 1916 remained and, indeed, remains to this day.

Bonar Law, a man utterly unknown to his homeland, in a few short years set the political agenda in Britain for the next eighty years and perhaps longer.

Canadians should know these things.

PROPORTIONAL REPRESENTATION:
HAS ITS TIME FINALLY ARRIVED?

Following Canadian political matters can be frustrating, so frustrating in fact that most sensible people read the sports pages instead.

You see, the system is phoney from top to bottom and nothing can be done except complete and utter change. The system of "responsible government" worked for the British when they imposed it on us centuries ago and it continues to work for them today, though many complaints we hear here about a presidential prime minister are heard there as well. But we royally screwed it up here in Canada. And when you look back on it, that was bound to happen. Canada isn't like Britain. For one thing Canada has two major linguistic groups. For another Canada has some major geography, so much in fact, that Canada's tenth prime minister, William Lyon Mackenzie King, once lamented in a speech to the House of Commons in 1936, "If some countries have too much history, we have too much geography." In Canada, once the party system took hold in about the 1880s, it became clear that for a party to govern, discipline had to be ironclad. There could be no disputed issues about language or region. They would split the government and let in the Opposition—always the "bad guys." That would never do.

For a long while the hard edge of party discipline was softened by the policies of Mackenzie King, who went to considerable pains to see that outer regions were represented in cabinet by strong men such as Jimmy Gardiner and Jimmy Sinclair, Pierre Trudeau's father-in-law. But Mr. Trudeau, who talked a fine democratic game, acted as an autocrat whenever he felt like it.

Trudeau discovered that all he had to do to win government was secure votes in Ontario and Quebec and the rest of the country could—and did—go to hell. Party discipline became easy to enforce when all MPs came from Central Canada. They all wanted to keep governing and were delighted to keep quiet in exchange for the lolly going to their ridings in Ontario and Quebec, where their voters live.

Over the years the prime minister developed sharp tools of discipline. Because he controlled appointments to cabinet he also controlled all government appointments from Supreme Court judges down to local enumerators. The prime minister controlled which MPs in the party would go on what parliamentary committees and it was a short step from there to telling those committees what they would discuss and what they would decide. As if he needed more power, the prime minister achieved the statutory power to approve the nomination papers of his party hopefuls. He was thus able to keep mavericks from getting party support at election time. Of all the powers the prime minister has, this is the most effective, for it is the one thing all MPs know about and don't need any reminding of. It's the ultimate whip.

As a consequence, Parliament is a sham. There is no debate because the decisions are made beforehand, usually by nameless unelected faces in the prime minister's office. Regions and constituencies have their say only behind the closed doors of a caucus or cabinet room. Since nothing is ever revealed, the constituent is left with the MP's assurance that he "really went to bat." This has resulted, it will come as no surprise, in a strong disconnection between government and the governed.

Changing from so-called "responsible government" to one in which the executive and the legislature are separated would bring power and dignity to the MP. It would force the executive to actually plead with Parliament for money in order to run the country. That would put considerable braking power over the executive in the hands of the legislature. And it would still leave the leader with considerable power, as is demonstrated by the office of the president of the United States.

Another way to break the stranglehold of party discipline is to change to a system of proportional representation. Nick Loenen's fine book *Citizenship and Democracy: A Case for Proportional Representation* (Dundurn, 1997) reviews the permutations and combinations of proportional representation. Under the pure proportional representation system, though, each party puts forward a list of candidates in descending order of party favour. Each party gets the number of MPs elected that corresponds to the percentage of popular vote they received. The immediate advantages of this are two: first, nearly always all parties would have some representation from all regions. Second, there would almost certainly be a minority government. Under proportional representation then, at least in theory, issues would truly have to be debated, since no government would be assured of a majority on any vote.

The drawbacks of proportional representation—or at least what opponents see as drawbacks—are several. The proportional representation government is said to be weak because there is seldom a majority. But should policy that actually has to pass a majority of MPs who represent the majority of voters be considered weak just because it isn't crammed down the throats of the minority? Can it be stated as a rule that tough, fast executive decisions are better policy than those that worked their way through the democratic process? I think not.

Another drawback to proportional representation is that the system breeds parties from the lunatic fringe. Israel being a notable exception, most countries with a system of proportional representation have a floor that must be reached—usually between two and five percent—before a party gets MPs elected. Second, why shouldn't single-issue parties have a parliamentary voice, however small? In a country that professes to be democratic shouldn't all points of view be represented in Parliament? The consequence of our present "first past the post" system is that the band of dissent is very narrow, with the major parties often agreeing, without saying so, not to discuss certain issues, such as abortion, for example.

My major concerns about the system of proportional representation are two. The system would have to be run on a province-by-province basis. Otherwise the major parties' lists would include only those who favour the Central Canadian bias. In a country as big and diverse as Canada no constituencies would be left, a result that would be quite unsatisfactory to most Canadians, especially those who live outside Central Canada. That should pose no problem—the party lists are simply lists of provincial MPs. Second, party lists are prone to represent the party faithful, the donors, bagmen and hacks who, once elected, have no allegiance to anyone but the party brass. That's a tougher problem and may require legislation mandating that party members be involved in selecting the list. The New Zealand experience of proportional representation seems to have been that, as the system matures, the problem of allegiance to party brass disappears. If the party list was one general list for the entire country, not one broken down into separate provincial lists, the danger, a real one, is that national parties would only have Central Canadians or Canadians who were centrists, on that list. On the other hand, if there were in fact ten separate elections, one in each province, with candidates selected by provincial wings of the parties, presumably each party would feel compelled to put forward candidates that province would see as representing their interests.

There are solutions, of course. New Zealand as well as Germany has partial proportional representation in which 50 percent of MPs are elected off "lists" and 50 percent are elected in constituencies in the traditional manner of "first past the post" governments. (New Zealand isn't quite 50-50 because they have four seats allotted to Maoris who elect off a special list.)

I go no further on the topic because it starts to get complicated. In my view, however much a system of proportional representation may leave much to be desired, it is by far better than the "first past the post" system we have now. There is no perfect system; we can only seek a better one.

But here is where my frustration lies. In Canada we can't even debate the change much less see the reform. Why not? Simple. What government, elected under a "first past the post" system and given the dictatorship of that system, is going to reform the system so that they lose absolute and perhaps all power?

Yes, it was done in New Zealand, a small unitary state with very little regional jealousy. There they had two referenda, one to decide if change was wanted and the second, after the answer was yes, to select the system. The strong desire to change came when in 1978 and 1981 a government was elected with fewer popular votes than the party in second place. New Zealand might give heart to provinces that want to reform their own systems. But can you seriously contemplate Jean Chrétien or Paul Martin bringing in a system that would loosen the Liberal Party's grip on the throat of Canada?

You see, there is another joker in the Canadian deck and it's called the amending formula to the constitution. Even if you could bring in amendments that only required seven of the ten provinces plus Ottawa to agree to change, by a 1995 Commons resolution, passed in February 1996, Ottawa has agreed to veto any proposition any of the five regions oppose. This means that not only is reform impossible but private debate is useless. For why go to the trouble of getting up a head of steam when nothing can ever come of your efforts? Political realities mean Parliament won't amend current legislation to change to a system of proportional representation.

Thus the frustration. And thus we Canadians stumble along, run by a five-year dictator who tells his cowering caucus what to do and we're unable to do a damned thing about it.

Who's Minding the Store?

Through abuse of the party system and the electoral laws, the prime minister has grabbed all the power unto his office. Because the government can fall on an adverse vote, the prime minister has been able to enforce party discipline. After all, who wants to lose an election?

The prime minister not only has it in his power to dispose promotions and gifts, he can also refuse to give party approval to any MP's nomination. He has the power of political life and death over his caucus. That's only one of a pair of catastrophes that have been the death knell to our parliamentary system.

The other catastrophe is that the prime minister no longer even bothers to ask Parliament for money. He simply takes it. In fact he doesn't even bother going through the motions of presenting a budget, having the budget estimates examined by Parliament, and then obtaining parliamentary approval. He simply has his captive caucus pass interim supply from time to time as is required.

These are outrages and most populations would be up in arms for half the aggravation. But Canadians love authority and like to believe that their leaders have the public's best interest at heart and thus shouldn't be criticized too loudly.

But a growing number of Canadians is getting more than just a little perturbed and they're asking what they can do.

First, the problems. The House of Commons is made up of one man who matters, the prime minister, and 300 who don't. This is not hyperbole; it's true. The 300 are divided among Opposition members who can verbalize their constituents' concerns but no more than that and the government members who do exactly what the whips tell them to do. The whips are, of course, directly answerable to the prime minister.

The second problem in Canada is our parliamentary system. We tried to graft an American notion, a senate, onto a lower House of Representatives by population so as to have democracy spread equally across the country. Of course we didn't really graft the American notion. That would have given real representation to regions. We just pinched the name.

What we have is a senate that outrages all who are victims to it and a lower house in which half plus one of its members have 100 percent of the power. That bare majority is tightly controlled by the prime minister personally and on the advice of his unelected cabal in the Prime Minister's Office (P.M.O.) mostly from the central provinces. Party discipline is ironclad and power is entirely top down. While the theory is that the House of Commons holds the executive accountable—the theory of "responsible" government—the very opposite is the case.

What, then, are the possible solutions?

Divorcing the executive from the legislative, in other words a republican system, is one possible solution. But this remedy may be too much for the patient. Let me offer some other solutions that are almost cost free and wouldn't require any amendments to our quite unamendable constitution.

Let's start with the shape of our legislatures. Churchill once said, wisely, "First we shape our buildings, then our buildings shape us." Our legislatures, with the exception of Manitoba, have cross benches where MPs glare and shout at each other according to party and where the government cheering section reminds one of well-trained applauding seals. I suggested in *Canada: Is Anyone Listening?* (Key Porter, 1998) that we reconstruct our chamber into a horseshoe shape with a podium for the MP with the floor and that members be seated alphabetically according to constituency. This will give a feeling and measure of collegiality and cordiality where there is now vicious deadlock.

Then members of Parliament need to seize back their ancient rights and privileges. In the beginning, Parliament was a collection of men who represented interests, which later became geographical areas called constituencies. As majority rule prevailed, not unnaturally those with similar views banded together to form an executive, or cabinet. It could be altered, both by the prime minister (and the monarch in earlier days) or even dismissed if they displeased the majority. As the party system evolved in Britain in the eighteenth century the notion of party discipline developed so that executives, that is to say, the cabinet, could have some security of tenure. From that developed the notion that governments would fall upon an adverse vote and a new one put in its place, now invariably after an election.

Prime ministers soon learned that if they wanted to stay in power, they must develop "sticks and carrots" to discipline their executive. The biggest stick was party support at election time. As matters progressed it became virtually impossible for a candidate to win as an independent. He had to have the money, prestige and formal backing that came with party affiliation if he wanted any chance for victory.

Members of Parliament had another way to control the cabinet: the parliamentary committee, which, in effect, "shadowed" various departments of government. If, for example, the finance minister was thought to be misspending public money he could be hauled before the finance committee and held to account. It wasn't long before prime ministers came to the conclusion that this wasn't necessarily a good idea. They used their "sticks" to decide which government MPs would be appointed to sit on committees and which would be appointed to chair the committee and therefore determine its agenda.

Here, then, are one or two "modest proposals" for the return of power and dignity to the MP. First, repeal section 67(4)(c) of the Canada Election Act thus eliminating the power of the leader of a party to approve the candidacy for Parliament. Simply require, on penalty of perjury, that a candidate file an affidavit saying that he has been duly and properly nominated by whatever the constituency organization is of whatever party. This would bring party leaders back to earth in a big way. It wouldn't eliminate the power of party leaders. Of course, the opposition of a leader to a candidacy would still carry great weight. But it would free up constituency organizations and make it harder for the leader to interfere in local matters or even, as is the practice of the current prime minister, "parachute" candidates into a riding.

Second, Parliament must demand and receive the right to appoint its own committees. The various caucuses would select committee members on the secret vote of its members. Similarly, committee chairs would be selected by secret ballot of the newly selected committee. When you think about it, it's outrageous (but so very Canadian) that we permit the prime minister, the person who is to be held to account, to select those who would evaluate his performance.

Third, upon the vote of, say, 30 percent of those voting, a vote in the House of Commons would be by secret ballot. This suggestion always brings shrieks of horror at the thought that our MPs would not vote up front where we could see how they voted. But we now know precisely how MPs, especially in the government, vote. They vote as their leader tells them to vote. They do that no matter what the dictates of their conscience, no matter what their constituents might wish. If Parliament brought in this rule to govern its own affairs it would seldom if ever be used. What government would risk putting to a vote something that didn't have the real approval of its members? Some might say that a "free vote" is what's required but in a "free vote" the leader watches the way people vote. Those of his MPs who don't vote as directed are subject to all the penalties the leader can impose.

These three changes are not easy to make only because there is not the will to make them. From a technical point of view they are a lead pipe cinch. It is only because those who hold power will do no more than pay lip service to real change plus the fact that MPs refuse to jeopardize their seats and, if they obey their leader, their prospects, that what is no more than an assertion by Parliament of their rights and privileges won't happen.

But let it not be said that they can't happen.

B.C. Separation and the Constitutional Veto

I have always wanted Canada to survive, but I no longer believe it can and I now I hope that British Columbia goes it alone as a viable and wealthy country of its own.

I have learned—and I admit that I'm a slow learner—that my version of Canadian identity doesn't jibe with the official version. Because I don't subscribe to the establishment's accepted Canadian catechism that Canada is the tension between Upper Canada and Lower Canada and that all else is merely a sideshow, I'm badly out of step.

The debate for B.C. separation must begin and it must be out in the open. It's time for British Columbians to contemplate seriously an existence outside of Canada.

I suppose the straw that broke the camel's back for me was the softwood lumber crisis, which saw what was a bread and butter issue in British Columbia treated so casually an Ontarian, Pat O'Brien, parliamentary secretary to the Minister for International Trade, who opined at the height of the dispute in November 2001 that there were some "nervous Nellies" among the softwood lumber industry in British Columbia. He said this at the very moment that thousands of B.C. lumber workers were being laid off, many permanently. This stupid remark betrays so vividly the typical Central Canadian attitude towards British Columbia, an attitude that is said and acted out all the time in so many different ways and has been extant since Confederation. Moreover, this attitude speaks to the larger issue: Is it worth British Columbia's while, culturally, sentimentally or economically, to stay in Canada?

Let me open the discussion by asking yet another question: Shouldn't British Columbia first attempt to deal with its grievances within the federation of Canada? Should we not, as loyal Canadians, simply accept the rule of the majority, however oppressive that rule may be? I say no for a very good reason and I hope that you will remember this essay, if you remember it at all, for this statement:

> There is no way the Canadian Constitution can ever be changed unless Central Canada agrees. Since everything British Columbia wants, and is entitled to, means a diminution of Ontario and Quebec power, changes will never, ever be agreed to. Never.

Yes, there is, within the constitution, a provision by which some changes can be made by agreement of 50 percent of the population representing seven provinces, plus the federal government. But Jean Chrétien dashed even that glimmer of hope in December 1995 when he caused Parliament to pass a resolution under which Ottawa would, if any of the five regions so demanded, reject a constitutional amendment. That effectively gave both Quebec and Ontario a veto over every change ever proposed. (It is glibly argued that since British Columbia also has this ersatz veto the province should be satisfied, but of course British Columbia wants amendments, not vetoes. A veto is the tool, and a very effective one, of the status quo.)

Constitutions must be capable of amendment, otherwise there is no hope for those who feel aggrieved. They must not be amended easily, otherwise uncertainty prevails. What a constitution can never have, if it is to function, is a veto for any constituent part of the society it governs. Allowing a veto ensures constitutional constipation, for no one every gives up power voluntarily.

Change within Canada that would remedy the grievances of British Columbia is impossible. Worse than that, much-needed reforms to the way Canada governs itself will never happen. With the constitution as it stands, no matter what party is in office, Quebec and Ontario will run this country precisely as they please forevermore. Constitutional changes won't be aired because no one will discuss something that can't possibly happen.

The Central Canadian vision of Canada will always prevail because, no matter how badly Central Canada is outnumbered, nothing can ever change without the consent of both Ontario and Quebec. They have a constitutional veto and we are forever burdened with their view of Canada.

Some other things will never happen.

There will be no fair representation in the House of Commons for British Columbia. We will always be grossly under-represented because, by operation of statute, no province can fall below the number of MPs it had in 1978. This means that provinces with falling populations gain, proportionally, while growing provinces fall behind. The only hope is that Ontario, which also loses seats by this insane formula, will see the light and push for fair play.

There will be no change to the Supreme Court of Canada. No matter what population changes happen, six out of nine Supreme Court judges will always come from Ontario and Quebec, with at least three from Quebec and probably one French Canadian from outside that province. The Supreme Court will continue to be appointed by the prime minister who will always now be from Quebec or a dear ally. For example, in 1997, Michel Bastarache, a French speaker from New Brunswick, was appointed to the Supreme Court of Canada. And what was the principal reason Prime Minister Chrétien gave? That Mr. Bastarache was a loyal Canadian as proved by the fact that he had co-chaired the national Yes Committee for the Charlottetown Accord Referendum. Think on this. The prime minister of Canada has determined that the litmus test for loyalty in this country is whether you voted for Charlottetown. Where does that leave the nearly 70 percent of British Columbians who voted no?

It leaves us knowing that only centrist minded, politically safe appointments will be made to the Supreme Court. Do we in British Columbia want to call upon such a Supreme Court to decide whether it is British Columbia or Ottawa that controls the oil and gas rights in Hecate Strait, for example?

Further, there will be no upper house with proper regional representation, much less anything remotely representing an elected, equal and effective Senate. Quebec won't stand for it and that ends that. The only way they will ever allow Senate change to happen is if compensatory power is given Ontario and Quebec (as Charlottetown proposed) thus increasing their stranglehold on control and destroying the whole point of having a regional upper house to offset the dictatorship of a majority all located in one place.

There will be no reform of the way the prime minister runs the House of Commons as a personal fiefdom where he is the feudal lord of the manor. There will be no power to the parliamentary committees much less power to individual MPs because that would weaken the way Central Canada controls the prime minister, who controls Parliament. It goes without saying that there will be no reform of the election process such as proportional representation or a variation thereof. (You will remember that when Chrétien was set to topple the Tories in 1993 he promised that after the election proportional representation would be the top item on his agenda. The words haven't passed his lips since.)

There could well be Charlottetown revisited within a year of Jean Charest winning the next Quebec election. We will be told, in British Columbia, that we must, as good Canadians, support a special status for Quebec, a permanent Quebec veto over all constitutional amendments and a permanent 25 percent of the House of Commons for Quebec, regardless of population shifts in the country. The inevitable and ongoing distortions this will present will be to the ever-increasing disadvantage of British Columbia. They will be pooh-poohed, just as they were by Joe Clark and Brian Mulroney in 1992 at the time of Charlottetown.*

* It is time, of course, to start considering what Quebec's constitutional position will be if Mario Dumont and his ADQ pull off an electoral upset.

The long and the short of it politically is that British Columbia, if it stays in Canada, must endure a system which will evermore and increasingly be dominated by Central Canada, where the prime minister must be French Canadian or at least speak French. As W. A. C. Bennett said so well thirty years ago, "British Columbia will ever be a goblet to be drained by the East."

British Columbians have the right, perhaps even the duty to future generations, to examine their place in a federation where the government not only doesn't give a damn about them but, much worse, has no reason to politically.

The notion of a British Columbia separate from Canada is not new. It started before the ink on the Act of Union was dry. With the debate comes the question of British Columbia's options, aside from enduring permanent and serious inequity. Many ideas abound. What about joining the three western provinces, perhaps with the Yukon thrown in? Wouldn't that be the bee's knees? We would have everything: lumber, minerals, grain, meat, dairy products, coal, oil and gas and warm water ports served by railways. What country could ask for anything more?

Like so many things that sound too good to be true, it is. What would be the national glue to hold such a country together? For Canada, and I speak only half facetiously, it's our love-hate relationships with Quebec and Ontario. But what on earth do The Pas, Manitoba, and Ucluelet, British Columbia, have in common? In British Columbia we are as divided from the Prairie provinces, and they from us, as we are from Central Canada and Atlantic Canada. British Columbia has quite a different history for one thing. Our people got here quite differently and it shows to this day as you hear the faint English accent of Oak Bay and the faint Ukrainian accent of Edmonton. Our economies are vastly different and they have shaped our different cultures. Moreover, mountain chains divide us both literally and figuratively. Perversely, the figurative division of which I speak is demonstrated by the British Columbia Peace River District, which lies to the east of the Rockies. With modern transportation, that shouldn't mean anything, but it does. Many B.C. Peace River dwellers feel closer to Albertans than they do to their provincial brethren.

But there's a bigger problem than cultural differences and that is politics. How would you govern such a country? British Columbia has more people than any of the Prairie provinces and, as people leave Manitoba and Saskatchewan, often for British Columbia, and B.C.'s population increases, British Columbia would be the dominant partner. Indeed, as Alberta's population continues to grow, the two easternmost Prairie provinces would be more and more politically marginalized. If you lived in a Prairie province how would you like being governed by a government controlled by British Columbia and Alberta, two rich provinces? In fact, paradoxically, when you think about it, the problem gets worse if you drop either Saskatchewan or Manitoba or both from the equation for then British Columbia really dominates on the basis of population.

Having arrived at some sort of constitution, how would the four provinces amend it? By three to four vote? Does anyone really believe that British Columbia would grant unto its three eastern neighbours the power to amend, against its wishes, the constitution of the new country? You would find British Columbians in a new country about as enthusiastic about giving up power to an upper house as Ontario and Quebec are now.

No, British Columbia may find it necessary to make new arrangements, especially if Quebec should secede, but a union with the three Prairie provinces simply isn't an option.

We must discuss our future but we would be most unwise to base our thoughts on anything other than the country of British Columbia. If there are to be other arrangements, let them happen as they will. In the meantime we have quite enough on our plates without buying into new federal arrangements that promise to be as troublesome as the ones we have now.

THOUGHTS FOR AN
INDEPENDENCE DAY

July 4, Independence Day, when the bands are playing and the
firecrackers are popping below the border, is a good time to
think about the giant eagle with the big wings that lives to the
south of us.

Canada's relationship with the United States has always been
prickly, going back to the time of the United Empire Loyalists,
who, during and immediately after the American Revolutionary
War, fled to Canada to retain their loyalty to the British Crown.
But, much as we may from time to time wish it to be otherwise,
the United States is with us, as a physically attached neighbour—
always has been and always will be.

We have resisted "Manifest Destiny" up to a point. In 1846
we gave away the State of Washington, which should have been
ours. We resisted expansionist President James Polk's cry of
"Fifty-four Forty or Fight!", which meant that he was willing to
fight Britain for possession of Oregon north to the 54°40' paral-
lel. This would have given the United States possession of British
Columbia north to the southern tip of Alaska. Hush up, you in
the back row, who are saying, "More's the pity."

The Canadian image of the predatory Yankee was summed up
by Thomas Haliburton's imaginary Yankee clockmaker, Sam
Slick, who travelled through Nova Scotia towns and villages
selling his clocks and spouting "wise-saws," which were
Haliburton's views of the government and the needs of the people. His satirical accounts became universally popular in the
early part of the nineteenth century and created an image of
Americans that became part of the Canadian psyche, preventing

free trade in 1911 and postponing it until 1990.

Now, it seems to me, we're being asked to re-evaluate our relationship.

NAFTA has been a success—not an unqualified success but a success for all that. Trade with the United States and Mexico, our two partners, is up enormously. Canadian direct investment in NAFTA countries has also increased, reaching $154 billion into the United States in 2000, a 127 percent increase over the 1993 level, and $3.2 billion into Mexico, more than six times the pre-NAFTA level. Our jobs have not all vanished to Mexican peons along the Rio Grande. What the experts said would happen did. Mexico is not only becoming more prosperous, it is actually becoming democratic. To the great surprise of the hard left it is actually doing something about working conditions and the environment.

One thing the left has said—and very loudly—is true: there has been a loss of Canadian sovereignty. And more will be lost. What we tend to forget is that this loss cuts three ways. There is a loss of sovereignty in both the United States and Mexico, where people are complaining bitterly. The fact remains that every time a country agrees to forbear a national right, signs any sort of international treaty or undertaking, it loses some sovereignty.

What we also tend to forget is that Canadians have far more capital invested in the United States than Americans have invested in Canada. The Americans generally have much more foreign ownership to howl about than Canadians do. Indeed, Canada enjoys a $60 billion trade surplus with America.

The talk now is of extending NAFTA to the so-called "southern cone" to include Chile, Argentina, Uruguay and Brazil. The expansion will happen despite the Council of Canadians and what's left of the left.

What will it mean? Almost certainly it means that we will all use the American dollar resulting in an additional loss of sovereignty. It will make sense to have one currency for such a huge trading partnership and that currency of choice will surely be the Yankee dollar, just as the euro has come to almost all of the European Community, excluding Britain. Britain's foot-dragging on throwing out the pound for the euro reflects concerns similar to those of Canadians. Can a country using another country's currency maintain more than token sovereignty? After all, the original reason for a Parliament was to control the king's purse. The loss of that power would surely emasculate the Canadian government. With the euro, at least Britain is still a big player in the mechanisms of government. Canadians would be kidding themselves to think that the U.S. Congress would surrender any of its power over the "greenback." Associated with this fear is the knowledge that fiscal policy would be set in Washington with Americans not Canadians in mind. British Columbia has had many grievances with Ottawa's fiscal policy about which it can do little. How would British Columbians like a monetary policy that is set in Washington, a government over which it would have zero influence?

It seems to me that we are wasting a great deal of our national energy. It's not as if our "democratic" way of life is threatened—we are a democracy in name only as it is. What we should be concerned about is retaining our social values, articulated in such things as medicare, employment insurance and workers' compensation. We must guard our ability to be more than hewers of wood and carriers of water for the United States, although perhaps those in Western Canada have already become used to that role. We will be suppliers of natural resources to the United States, and the world, for a long time to come. But we must do that with care and in conjunction with broadening our economy beyond this. In other words, while we will always be suppliers of natural resources we shouldn't let that prevent us from adding value to those resources before they are exported.

It's not too late—though grossly impractical—to opt out of NAFTA. Many Canadians would like to give notice and leave. If we do, Canada voluntarily becomes a trade orphan. NAFTA will grow without us, as will other trade organizations growing in

Europe and Asia. At least two Asian groupings are in the works, though in the early formative stages. Australia and New Zealand, already in what they call Closer Economic Relationship (CER), are looking for partners in Southeast Asia. China and Japan, either together or separately, are making noises about new market partnerships. I don't say that people will refuse our products, just that they will not be preferred much less protected.

These are times of enormous change. It's time Canadians debated these proposed changes instead of either demonstrating against what we fear they'll be, or sitting on our hands assuming that Big Daddy in Ottawa knows what's best for us.

CAN THE "RIGHT"
EVER UNITE?

Since the demise of the federal Tories in 1993 there has been the cry to "unite the right." It was assumed that the vehicle for right-wing unity had been found with the development of the Reform Party in the late 1980s and throughout the 1990s and then its reinvention as the Canadian Alliance in April 2000. But the elections of 1997 and 2000 demonstrated that this vehicle had failed. In both elections the Tories and Reform cum Alliance split the vote in Ontario, permitting the Liberals to win. "Unite the right" again became the cry of the defeated.

I detect a major flaw in the notion of a united right and it may be because of my own politics. I do not consider myself a right-winger at all. Were it not for the disgraceful behaviour of the Liberal Party during the October Crisis in 1970 and their subsequent discovery that they could win the country without considering the western half of it, I would still be a Liberal. I suppose I'm the true middle-of-the-roader—a conservative fiscally and on the left socially.

Yet I supported the Reform–Alliance in three elections. Why? Certainly not because of the anti-Semitic, gay bashing, racist feelings of too many of its members. No, I supported the Reform–Alliance because they promised what I thought were necessary reforms to the system. I was in tune with their ideas on how Canada ought to govern itself.

Now unity of the Canadian Alliance and the Conservative parties is proposed. How many Canadians like me find any proposed right-wing coalition philosophically abhorrent? A unified party of the Canadian Alliance and the Conservatives would have a big problem. The Conservatives would appease Quebec with a distinct society and constitutional favouritism. Joe Clark is an unrepentant Meechkin who believes some provinces should be more equal than others. I couldn't support much less belong to such a party.

Like Humpty Dumpty, the Canadian Alliance had a great fall when they rid themselves of Stockwell Day. Whether or not Harper will be able to hold the leadership much less make inroads east of the Lakehead and put Humpty Dumpty together again very much remains to be seen. What seems to be lost on everyone is that the party split was not just on ideological lines—Day and Harper are as alike as Tweedledum and Tweedledee. The split is as ideological as it is regional. British Columbia, the mainstay of the Alliance, is uncomfortable with the perceived "rednecks" in the Alberta wing. Ontario sees itself as the "lynchpin" of Confederation, while western Alliance members, whatever part of the political spectrum they occupy, see Ontario as the dragon to be slayed.

All political parties are coalitions but the long-established political parties in Canada traditionally have made all within the party feel comfortable. One of the most successful of British Columbia's coalitions, the Social Credit Party, managed for nearly forty years to sustain a political atmosphere in which Conservatives and Liberals could live together in reasonable harmony. But here, too, the split that fractured the party lay between the far right, very much including the religious right who were mostly in rural British Columbia, and the "red Tories" and Liberals of the city.

The similarities between Bill Vander Zalm of 1986 and Stockwell Day of 2001 are eerie. Both leaders came from the Christian right (even though Vander Zalm is Catholic he wowed them in the Fraser Valley Bible belt). Each leader is charismatic and each was selected because the party thought they could win. (Not that this isn't a serious consideration but it can be disastrous if it's the only one.) Both leaders came from outside the mainstream of the party, especially outside the parliamentary caucus.

Further similarities can be found in the two leader's approaches to the controversial issue of abortion. While Vander Zalm managed to keep from mentioning it in the 1986 campaign, he had scarcely got comfortable in his office before he had his Attorney General screaming at him on the subject of, yes, abortion, a federal responsibility. Stockwell Day made abortion an issue on the first day of his 2000 campaign. He also managed to badly divide the party on his leadership within a few months. In short, both Day and Vander Zalm demonstrated that there can be no successful "right-wing party" that favours the "right wing" over the moderates. Vander Zalm ruined himself and his party; Day ruined himself and his effect on the party remains to be seen.

While the Canadian Alliance holds out much hope for the leadership of Stephen Harper, and it's true that he won the leadership by defeating the Christian fundamentalists, he is much further to the right than the conservatives of both Ontario and British Columbia, where he must win.

Adherents to the "far right" can be found in both Ontario and British Columbia but both provinces tend to be pretty much middle of the road. Mike Harris is the exception that proves the rule and he is gone because, having served his purpose of show- ing he was not a wild spender like David Peterson or Bob Rae, became expendable in a province that wanted his short-term solutions but not his long-term politics.

With the exception of the Fraser Valley Bible belt, British Columbians are not so right wing as they are against Ottawa and the Liberals, which to them seem to be much the same thing. They are not especially right wing and although Liberals have not done well, federally, here for thirty years, that could change. Stephen Harper has to hope that British Columbians continue to support his party because they hate the Liberals. That's not a solid base for long-term party strength, though. Without British Columbia, there is no Alliance Party. Without Ontario, there is no victory.

Here, then, the problem comes into focus. Not only must Stephen Harper satisfy the right who elected him and the moderates who sustain him, he must somehow pacify the various regions. The Liberals have long been in the happy position (for them, though not the country) where they needed to pacify only two regions—Ontario and Quebec. The long and powerful influence of the party in Quebec sustained it there. Mr. Harper must not only satisfy the two western regions, the Prairies provinces and British Columbia (three regions if you count Alberta separately) but Ontario and, because Quebec seems out of reach, Atlantic Canada as well.

Ontario is a big nut to crack. It sees the universe unfolding a bit differently and is much more apt to view Canada as the never-ending struggle of Upper and Lower Canada with some outer fringes that make unpleasant noises from time to time. But I sense that more and more people in Ontario feel as I do—in favour of reform and sick to death of the Liberals. Yet they may well part from the Alliance on the Quebec question. Where the Alliance, reflecting its western roots, favours equality of all provinces I suspect that many Ontarians would appease Quebec long before they would stand in favour of any reforms that might upset her. The critical question is whether Ontarians, while seeing the injustice of the system, also realize they are the beneficiaries of that injustice and are still prepared to vote for reform. Rare indeed is the voter who votes out of altruistic motives.

But what about the Tories? Where is their role in all this? Stephen Harper has made it plain that they must join him and that he's the only game in town. Harper has no choice if he wants to keep his job. Neither British Columbia nor Alberta will vote for a party in which Joe Clark has serious influence. Uniting the "right" is still a reasonable prospect but uniting the two "right-wing parties" is an idea whose time has passed.

The Canadian Alliance still has a hope. To understand this one must go back through the mists of time to John Diefenbaker and forward to Brian Mulroney. Both men won massive majorities not because their party or they personally were terribly popular but because the Liberals self-destructed. The election of Stephen Harper as Alliance leader provided hope for the right however divided they may seem, for they are united on the important issue—how to get rid of the Liberals. Voters won't ask too many questions as they gleefully turf the Liberals from office using the only viable vehicle available, the Canadian Alliance. After all, by the next federal election the Liberals will have been in government continuously for nearly fifteen years.

It's a long shot. But, as Damon Runyan said, "The race is not always to the swift nor the battle to the strong, but that's the way to bet." If you like a long shot with a chance, put a loony on the Canadian Alliance—not a penny more, though.

AND A GAY TIME WAS
HAD BY ALL

The issue of homosexuality continues to beset some of our politicians. In the Canadian Alliance, in particular, while its official position is one of bare tolerance, the struggle takes place pretty darn near the surface. The more liberal members of the Alliance are of the "some of my best friends are" variety and from there it descends to outright hostility. Much of the grassroots membership of the party are well connected with evangelist Reverend Jerry Falwell's Moral Majority. Falwell preaches against homosexuality, no exceptions, and prides himself on having converted many gays to the "straight" life.

Put briefly, the Canadian Alliance so often seems to be against homosexuality and homosexuals because many Alliance politicians are against it but, more importantly, so is its core support in the religious community.

Many people, including myself, can't figure out what all the fuss is about. Different strokes for different folks. Live and let live. But the hostility against gays in the right-wing Christian community is white hot. They talk frequently of a "gay agenda," which evidently extends to the wholesale conversion of kids to this sinful lifestyle. Whenever I do radio programs on the subject I can be sure of an outraged response. An article I wrote for *WestCoast Families* magazine on the subject brought enormous outrage from people who were convinced that the paper, in using my column, was giving in to this mysterious, but pervasive "gay agenda."

I have trouble understanding the source of this hostility. Is it the typical puritanical arm of Christianity's dislike of pleasure of any kind? Is it the glumness we associate with drippy-nosed,

Presbyterian preachers who derive from the tee-totalling Lowlands of Scotland?

The case these people make is that Leviticus 18:22 and 20:13 forbid man having sex with man as one would with a woman. This is brought into Christianity, according to them, when Jesus, who was silent on the subject of homosexuality, exhorted his followers to obey the laws of God as set down by the prophets, especially Moses, who is also silent on the subject.

But Leviticus doesn't forbid homosexuality, just sodomy. He says nothing about oral sex or mutual masturbation, for example. And he says nothing whatever about lesbianism. This has led some Biblical scholars to conclude that Leviticus was not an injunction against male homosexual practices on moral grounds but reflected health concerns.

One has to assume that homosexuality was as prevalent in Old Testament times and during the life of Christ as it is today. Indeed, in contemporary Greek and Roman societies it was quite accepted. That being the case, why doesn't Leviticus forbid all homosexual practices? And why no injunction against lesbianism? Of greater interest, why is it not one of Moses' Ten Commandments? Surely, if homosexuality were as sinful as right-wing Christians proclaim, it would be as bad if not worse than adultery, for example, or coveting one's neighbour's wife or ass (the animal, that is). And why wouldn't Christ have been very specific about it? Surely if the sin, if it be so, is such that right-wing Christians all but set their hair on fire at the thought of it, they must have more to go on than references to verses in Leviticus which only forbid male homosexuality. Christ did not spend time debating the subject in his ministry. Christ was concerned that we love God, our neighbour and ourselves, upon that hung all the law and the prophets.

I am a profoundly heterosexual Christian and must say that I dissociate myself from those of my co-religionists who get excited on the matter. I think the questions of gay marriages or the blessing of gay unions does present some interesting theological disagreements. My church, the Anglican Church, is going through considerable discomfort on that very subject. But how the subject can cause such anguish to the Christians who so easily support the Canadian Alliance is beyond me.

I may not love the lifestyle but I do love the homosexual as my neighbour. I would contend that that's what the teachings of Jesus were all about.

Is Big Brother Watching
You—And Telling?

The government of Canada now has about 2,000 bits of information on every adult Canadian and federal Privacy Commissioner Bruce Phillips is mad as hell, and so he should be. He has urged the government to dismantle this database of information, called the Longitudinal Labour Force File (LLFF), which contains data compiled from tax returns, child tax benefit payments, welfare files, federal job programs, job training and employment services, employment insurance files, and the nation's health insurance master file. This violation of privacy rights in Canada is the culmination of government abuses that go back many decades.

The modern census started in the United States whose government has that right entrenched in its constitution. And while a census was originally a pretty harmless thing, since it counted people and gave the government some sort of notion as to how large an army it could muster, the Canadian version has, since about 1966, become ever more prying into citizens' private affairs. My argument is that privacy, in and of itself, is a fundamental right of free people.

When the Canada Pension Plan was proclaimed on January 1, 1966, we were advised by no less a personage than Prime Minister Lester Pearson himself that all information disclosed would be confidential, just a teeny, weeny little secret between us and our government. The same with the Social Insurance Number (SIN) when it was introduced in 1964 in preparation for the Canada Pension Plan. Now you can scarcely buy a chocolate bar without having to disclose your SIN number.

Because of technological advances it is possible to collate all public information and all private information on a single file. Everything from the amount of your mortgage, how well you pay your bills, what political party you have supported, whether or not you've ever had a dose of clap and how many toilets are in your house are all bits of information the government has on your file.

Our census forms have gotten longer and longer. The 2001 Census even wanted to know how many loos are in your house or, indeed, if perhaps you have an outdoor privy. Every tenth citizen completed an even longer form of census, which many Canadians simply refused to fill out, possibly because for the first time it asked you to snitch on your neighbour. Hundreds of Canadians refused to answer these unbelievably intrusive questions but to my knowledge, no prosecutions followed.

Under the Income Tax Act whatever information you give Customs and Revenue Canada is privileged and cannot, under any circumstances, be disclosed to anyone else. That's what the government tells us. And why wouldn't you trust your government?

Well, for one thing the government can sell these files. So far, there is no evidence of actually selling the information but it's commonplace for government departments and agencies to give out broad demographic information to private industry through Statistics Canada. Private industry financially supports political parties.

Why is it, do you suppose, that you get *Elm Street* magazine in your Toronto *Globe and Mail* while the family across town does not? Someone has told *Elm Street* how much money people in your neighbourhood make and the marketers act accordingly.

Government also accumulates information on us because bureaucrats are congenital snoops. There is never the slightest curiosity in a bureaucrat that isn't reflected in a question that must be answered.

Now that this information is centralized, does anyone really believe that your secrets will be kept that way? Do you suppose for a second that when the police want information from your file that they'll be denied it unofficially if perhaps officially? And if they are being denied today, what about tomorrow?

Privacy Commissioner Bruce Phillips was right to be angry when knowledge of the Longitudinal Labour Force File database was revealed in 2000. Canadians across the country ought to be angry, too. We should be taking this matter up with our MPs, all but the Liberal ones, for you can be sure they'll just do as they always do, go along with their masters.

WHAT RIGHT TO ASSEMBLE?

Since September 11 the government has, in essence, taken away the sacred right of habeas corpus, the right to protection against unlawful detention, from those the police suspect of terrorist activities. As Canadians we love it, of course, just as we loved it when Pierre Trudeau brought in the War Measures Act in 1970 because an incompetent Quebec Provincial Police and an even more incompetent Quebec government couldn't deal with a couple of high profile kidnappings, one of which became a murder after the Act was invoked. Never mind that 433 of the 453 arrested were completely innocent people, incarcerated without the right to call their families, much less a lawyer (who couldn't have done anything anyway) and that even the kidnappers and murderers all but got away Scot free. Never mind that the entire country was put under martial law for something that happened in Quebec. Canadians lapped it up.

Freedom of assembly is one of the most sacred rights we possess along with freedom of speech. Freedom of assembly is what differentiates free societies from dictatorships. Freedom of assembly is also the freedom we seem too willing to give up when we don't like who is doing the assembling.

Before December 31, 1999—the night when people who can't count celebrated the millennium—Vancouver Police media liaison Constable Anne Drennan warned people not to come downtown unless they had a good reason. Think on that! It takes the breath away. The police are telling citizens that they must justify being on the Queen's highways. Yet, our population of freedom-loving Vancouverites murmured with contentment as often as with grumbles. My good reason was that I was going to assemble to celebrate because I damned well felt like it. I could walk where I pleased, except where the restriction is reasonable. In the end the public barely raised itself from its contented torpor and sort of agreed that Drennan might have overstepped the mark.

We assemble freely all the time and don't think about it. We go to church, play golf, attend annual meetings and that sort of stuff. We go to political gatherings where we plot the overthrow, albeit peacefully, of governments. Yet those and other innocent gatherings are the kinds of assembling that in some places in the world are against the law.

But what about the freedom to protest? We no longer think much about unions picketing places of business to further their claims for better wages and working conditions making it impossible, in the bargain, for the companies to do their business. We accept, and rightly so, the right of the worker to protest and to urge others to do the same. We protest the expansion of ferry facilities and no one suggests that this is wrong. We may disagree with the issue the protesters take but we indulge them their right. We watch with interest and often mixed feelings as people block roads, chain themselves to trees or run boats into the paths of whalers. We know that if they do so illegally they must suffer the consequences but we would never countenance authority preventing people from protesting, however goofy we might think their ideas.

When, however, the protesters are trying to interfere with politicians somehow we think differently. Those who protested the APEC economic leaders' meetings in Vancouver in November 1997 were protesting Canada getting down to serious business with international thugs masquerading as heads of state and heads of government. Some might not agree that places like Indonesia and China of that day were run by bad people, but a hell of a lot of people from all walks of life thought they were. Yet the police started arresting potential protesters days before the meeting, brutally arrested protesters for carrying cloth signs saying "Free Speech" and "Democracy" and then, with virtually no notice, pepper sprayed the crowds. To be fair, a lot of Canadians spoke out against this brutality but a hell of a lot didn't and far too many didn't think this sort of "assembly" ought to be permitted. Included in the last group were people such as the prime minister of Canada, the man charged with protecting our democratic rights. He and his ministers were up to their eyeballs in denying citizens the right to protest.

In April 2001 there was the huge and occasionally bloody protest in Quebec City against North and South American politicians debating closer economic ties and further widening of free trade and globalization. A lot of people, including me on occasion, see this globalization exercise as one in which large multinational corporations are almost totally free of government restraint, making decisions for us hitherto left to people we elect. Many see globalization as widening the gap between rich and poor and permitting the environment to be desecrated. There are, of course, lots of arguments in favour of freer trade but the point is that there are a dozen highly debatable issues involved. Under those conditions there is bound to be protest. Indeed without protest it would be almost absolute proof that we live in a dictatorship.

But, it is argued, the protest got out of hand just as it did in Vancouver, Seattle and Washington, D.C. Ah, then, is that the criterion? If the issues are of such universal importance that a lot of protesters from far and wide will want to make their views known, we will ban it? Or create a Berlin type wall around the politicians on the amazing assumption that this will not attract, like a moth to the flame, those who see such things in themselves as challenges to be met? Do we as a society say that union picket lines will be permitted and, indeed, respected even though there is often violence. On a matter of great principle, do we say that this great principle doesn't extend to protests against heads of government and heads of state making decisions over which we have no control? We don't, in short, ban union pickets because they are sometimes violent and are always to some degree threatening, nor should we. But should we ban peaceful picketing the high and the mighty because some thugs might show up?

It cannot be argued, of course, that because a woman dresses and acts provocatively her being raped is justified. It does, however, indicate a want of foresight.

A person who walks into an American inner city wearing gold chains and with a bulging wallet does not justify a mugging, but it does illustrate a want of care.

Similarly, the holding of a hugely controversial event in a most unsatisfactory place, where security is impossible, doesn't justify violence but it does indicate what, under those circumstances, must be seen as an arrogant indifference to obvious consequences.

All of this leads to what is the essential point that all seem to be missing. Protesters as well as those being protested against are entitled to the protection of the law. It follows that, because their right to peaceful protest might bring violence, banning the protest is not justified anymore than potential violence on a picket line justifies banning the right to picket.

Canadians, as a whole, don't defend our democratic rights. Police officers complain noisily when accused people "get off" (though one must note that, when police officers themselves are charged, they gravitate quickly to the very lawyers they detest the most). We complain bitterly about "criminals" getting legal aid. Many Canadians agreed with Constable Anne Drennan when she told people to stay home during the millennium celebrations unless they had a "good excuse." They also agreed with Drennan earlier when she and the mayor of Vancouver completely agreed with police officers wrongfully searching people for liquor and then confiscating it, even more illegally. Many thought it was quite okay in 1997 for the police to pick up a UBC student the day before the APEC economic leaders' meetings on a spurious charge and release him only on his undertaking not to protest. There was little, if any, public outcry when police beat up a young articled law student, whose "crime" was to display signs saying "Democracy" and "Free Speech."

Canadians love authority—our national creed is peace, order and good government. Democratic rights are things that get in the way. Any who think this is an accident should think again. We have an elected dictatorship in Canada, with members of Parliament who are merely high-paid flunkies of the prime minister's government. Canadians don't have democracy because they don't like the inconveniences that come with it.

SMOKERS' RIGHTS?

The issue of smoking in public places has largely been one of the forces of right against the forces of evil, when truly it is a question of civil rights. Those who, in what is now a lost cause, claim that their rights have been violated deserve an answer.

As I predicted publicly some years ago in an editorial on my morning radio program—I always advertise my successful predictions because there are so many of the other kind—the issue of smoking in public places would be settled as a matter of workers' compensation. It was unthinkable to me that the B.C. Workers' Compensation Board would not step in to curtail the very dangerous practice of forcing people to work in medically unsafe surroundings. The WCB decision was not, or perhaps I should say is not, final. This body, a quasi-judicial body mandated to protect the worker decided in 2000 that smoking would not be allowed in places people worked. In 2001, enter the Liberal government with a host of publicans to pay off for their electoral support and, despite their past bleatings about respecting the independence of the board, the Liberal government countermanded the WCB order and on January 16, 2002, announced new regulations effective May 1, 2002, to manage workers' exposure to second-hand smoke in B.C.'s hospitality industry. Smoking in bars and restaurants can now only take place in a separately ventilated room or on outdoor areas.

But the issue to me is broader, for I not only support a smoking ban but also the ban against advertising and go so far as to support a ban on all alcohol advertising. Let me pursue the last point for a moment. In 1976 I became British Columbia's

Minister of Consumer and Corporate Affairs and was responsible for the licensing and distribution of alcohol. At that time no advertising of any alcohol products on radio and television was permitted, by B.C. law. Until I left government in 1981 that remained the law despite constant lobbying, not by alcohol interests but by advertising firms and electronic media companies, which would greatly profit from advertising sold to television and radio broadcasters. After I left the ministry to lead the Ministry of Environment in 1978, in deference to my views and those of Bob McLelland, a prominent member of the Bill Bennett cabinet, the ban on beer and wine advertising continued. Shortly after I left government, in the spring of 1981, it was lifted.

How could I, a democrat and a liberal, oppose the advertising of a perfectly legal product? It was simple. The right of the advertiser to make money competed with the right of the public to maintain their health and that of their children. In deciding to disallow beer and wine advertising, my ministry didn't proceed on a whim or a cabinet minister's personal prejudice, we did research, lots of it. And to varying degrees it demonstrated two things: first, beer and wine advertising increased its consumption and, second, advertising clearly was geared to young people to ensure that the demand for alcohol moved from the older generation to the younger. Any fair-minded person, looking at the advertising proposed then (and which is now a reality), would agree that they advertise "lifestyle." It was all fun, with good-looking young people skiing or snowboarding or racing down a river or some other such attractive youthful pursuit. The dangers of alcohol were never mentioned. A young person who wanted to be "in" was never given the option not to drink. As legislators, we were being asked, therefore, to sanctify the advertiser's "right" to advertise, in a selective way, what is potentially a dangerous drug. And that point must be stressed. Alcohol is the most abused of all drugs and its abuse is our number one social problem. Government not only has the right but the duty to control the advertising of such a dangerous substance. And the same goes for tobacco.

Now back to the smoking ban. My first argument, then, is that the government has a duty to control harmful substances. My second argument is that smoking in a public place involves a competition of rights—your right to smoke and my right to be in a public place free of the discomfort but even more important the dangers of second-hand smoke. I do not deny you your right to smoke, only your right to force me to share it with you.

There are, forgive the pun, smokescreen arguments galore. Why not have better ventilation and allow pub owners to make their own rules? Why not allow liquor license holders to hire only staff who smoke? If you're going to go after second-hand smoke, why not get those trucks that spew noxious fumes into the atmosphere? And what about the homeowner who smokes and the plumber who comes into the house to fix the water pipes? Is that a breach of WCB regulations? And on the counterarguments go.

For one thing, it is no argument against eliminating an evil to say that there is a similar or worse evil somewhere else. You do what is possible. And you cannot restrict employment only to those who smoke. You cannot, in effect, say that smoking is a condition of employment. This is the old and thankfully discredited argument of the coal mine operator telling his miners that if they don't like the risks, go somewhere else. It was to avoid this sort of blackmail that factory and workers' compensation legislation came into the civilized workplace.

The Canadian Charter of Rights and Freedoms recognizes the right to restrain rights if to do so is consistent with a free country. The B.C. WCB ruling certainly complies with that. But essentially it gets down to this: The right to smoke cannot overrule the right of a citizen in a public place to breath air free from nicotine smoke. The argument is all but moot in Canada. Other countries are slow to follow but follow they will.

Perhaps I can coin an axiom to cover the situation: When rights compete, the right of the potential victim must always prevail.

POLITICAL BULLSHIT
AND ALL THAT

Politicians are generally considered to be shady people with little regard for the truth and a high regard for getting re-elected. It doesn't seem to ever occur to us that we are responsible for electing these people, time and time again, rather than looking for more honest replacements. The game of getting elected in Canada is crooked. Is it any wonder that the players are, too?

Unless you are tabbed for a safe constituency by Jean Chrétien, the first thing a prospective candidate must do is get the nomination for a constituency and that requires that you start a process of high flattery. You need a team and that team must convince party members, present as well as prospective, that you are the right person. The very last thing you do is take an unpopular stand. If your constituency thinks it's time for a new bridge across the local river or some such thing, you don't say, "Hold on, I think constituency 'X' has a better claim to highway money. Perhaps we should focus our attention elsewhere." No, siree, you come out foursquare for that bridge. You'll worry about your inability to deliver later. Besides, as Mr. Micawber hoped in *David Copperfield*, "Something might turn up."

Flattery, something you've perhaps never cared for very much, becomes second nature. People you hitherto detested get a forced smile, a brochure and maybe even a slap on the back and a "How're you doing, old buddy?"

If you want to win, your brochure will be a masterpiece of mindless excrement. You'll be in favour of better education for the kiddies, shortening of waiting lists in hospitals and safer streets. Whatever opinion you have on abortion will never escape your lips except perhaps, when you are backed into a corner and you say that while you have a very high regard for human life you would be reluctant to interfere, blah, blah, blah.

You will, of course, always be mindful of the constituency. Not for you the mindless following of a party line. Why, when you're elected you will be heard and your constituency will always come first. And, of course, you know or damned well ought to know that this is barnyard droppings.

You will meet groups of constituents with special interests and you will assure them that you support them all the way, even though you may have assured their worst enemies that you can see a lot in the case they make.

You will go to endless coffee parties, wine and cheese parties and public meetings on matters about which you couldn't care less. You will find yourself at city council meetings, oh so very concerned about what the city fathers and mothers are up to, even though you scarcely knew where city hall was before you entered your name for nomination. You will become a church attender for the first time since you were married and, if you have a clever campaign manager, you'll even get to read one of the lessons on a Sunday close to voting day. Moreover, assuming you are nominally a Christian, you will, with a high profile member of the appropriate community, visit any and all ethnic temples, tabernacles and synagogues in your area. And, of course, if the election is anywhere near Remembrance Day you will wangle a spot in the VIP parade.

Almost certainly at some public celebration during your campaign you will, with the enthusiasm of a schoolboy, set off fireworks, sing the national anthem, duck for apples, go carolling or do whatever the occasion demands.

Assuming you are nominated, you will do all the same things over again, except this time you will often have to make speeches. This requires some elegantly phrased mindless pap with suitable reference to everything you can think of that will please your audience.

Once elected, you are in for a rude awakening. You will find that, contrary to what you've been led to believe, no one really cares about what you think, unless, of course, it happens to be on the issue of the moment and your views coincide with those of the leader. It will become very clear to you that as former United States House of Representatives Speaker Sam Rayburn once said, "If you want to get along, go along."

If you happen to be a bit headstrong and inclined to do your own thing, you will either do as you're told or observe that nothing good happens to mavericks, only bad. Mavericks don't get into cabinet. Mavericks don't get good shadow cabinet posts if they're in opposition. Mavericks don't get to be speaker, or deputy speaker, or chair. Mavericks don't even get to be whip or deputy whip, and all these positions have perks and extra money attached. Only good little boys and girls who do as they're told, always patiently waiting for a pat on the head from the leader get to go on parliamentary committees that travel to neat places. Or they might really get lucky and get to go to a speaker's conference in Mauritius in the middle of our winter.

A week after you accepted the offer to seek a nomination, it's a miracle if you are still an honest person. But with all that sort of righteousness on your record, you have nothing to fear.

But let's not forget your old constituency. You'll find, especially if you happen to be a cabinet minister, that the people you fought for the nomination, whom you thought were loyal to you as the party's choice, have since they were defeated had a death wish for you and are now doing a spectacular job of stabbing you in the back.

You now find you must do two things, bullshit the folks along about how that bridge will be coming but these are tough times etcetera and continue all the social rambling you did as a candidate. You will speak at weddings, funerals and baptisms. You will spend most Saturday mornings cutting ribbons or going to constituency picnics or similar nauseating events. You will parade, pray, sing and talk yourself hoarse. You will become a master at speaking at fundraisers in terms that will have your red-necked audience happy while still appearing moderate later in print or on radio and television. You will ignore your family except insofar as they are dragged along to events and, in all likelihood, your marriage will falter if not fail. All the while you will manage tens of thousands of public words without ever uttering a phrase that is even remotely controversial. This means, in effect, that you bad mouth the other guys ad nauseum.

The whole exercise is play acting. The legislature itself is theatre. There is no debate because cabinet has already made the decision. All there is are some speeches you hope will get you some good ink. You do exactly what you're told and then try to persuade the people back home that you've been doing a hell of a job on their behalf.

Do I exaggerate? If anything, I understate the personal metamorphosis the ordinary person must go through to shed a private persona for a public one. You don't become a liar so much as a dissembler. You learn the political patois and how to shift your ground without anyone really noticing. You develop pat answers to expected questions. Indeed it is now the habit of first ministers' offices to send you written and oral bumph so that everyone sings from the same songsheet. You learn some of the fine arts such as appearing on a talk show and running out the clock so as to avoid having to dwell on unpleasant matters. Good politicians are good obfuscators.

Politics then is an art, and telling the whole unvarnished truth or anything remotely like it, is not part of the art form.

THE BIRTH AND DEATH
OF THE SOCREDS

The story of the Socred years in B.C. politics remains to be adequately told. There are good books, notably David Mitchell's *W. A. C. Bennett and the Rise of British Columbia* (Douglas & McIntyre, 1991), which tell part of the story very well. It is not my purpose here to write a complete history but to paint an impressionistic picture—a sort of tardy fin de siècle look back.

To understand what happens in B.C. politics it is necessary to understand British Columbia, which is living, ongoing proof of the saw that you can't escape your history. Perhaps the one piece of required reading for those who want to take the time to understand British Columbia is Jean Barman's *The West Beyond the West: A History of British Columbia* (University of Toronto Press, 1991), which lays out with admirable clarity the real story of how British Columbia came into being. From the outset British Columbia was an unruly place, indeed perhaps not a little bit anarchist. The people didn't arrive in one steady wave of immigration across what was then Canada. Instead, the first white people came across the continent and down our rivers, between 1792 and around 1825 to exploit the fur trade. These hardies were Hudson's Bay Company men who established places such as Fort Kamloops, Fort George (now Prince George), Fort Langley (briefly the capital of the united colony) and Fort Victoria, to name a few. Early British settlers started arriving in the mid-1800s travelling around the Horn. Later they came directly from Blighty via the new CPR passenger service. My maternal grandmother, a strong-willed Scottish Canadian from

Cape Breton Island, arrived on the second train. Law and order came in the person of the famous Matthew Baillie Begbie, an English barrister, often called "the hanging judge," a rather unfair sobriquet on the record but so widely used it stuck.

The Americans and Chinese came to strike it rich in the Cariboo gold rush in the early 1860s. But economic boom followed economic bust and by 1871, when Confederation was proposed, British Columbia was deep in debt. Entry into Confederation hardly came from love, then, but from two companion emotions: first, fear of absorption into the United States, which had in 1867 purchased Alaska and seemed to have set its sights on British Columbia, and, second, a need for money to pay for the building of the road to the Cariboo goldfields. As well, the dream of a transcontinental railway promised rich eastern markets for our substantial natural resources. In the event, the "confederationists" were successful in making a deal with the newly minted Canada whereby the national government paid our debt, promised to construct a national railway within ten years, and built some docks. The marriage, far from being one of love, was strictly one of convenience. (One of the more interesting of the "confederationists" was a man named William Smith who, under the multilingual name of Amor de Cosmos, founded the Victoria Colonist newspaper and was our second premier. Our first premier was the undistinguished unto anonymous John Foster McCreight.) Thus Confederation was a commercial act that carried with it the overtones of self-defence against the Yankees. This view has dominated the political scene in British Columbia ever since. There has scarcely been a premier, or indeed a provincial politician, who has not played the "Ottawa card" when seeking public approval. Seen as the "spoilt child of Confederation" by the hated east (not too strong a word I think), British Columbia has consistently lived up to the insult.

There are reasons this anti-Ottawa attitude has persisted over 131 years, not the least of which is the hearty reluctance of British Columbians to leave the province. For those from the "wet" coast, it is a dislike of winter. Whatever the reason, native British Columbians simply resist moving east whether to join the government or to move up the corporate ladder. Over the years, our MPs have often tended to be originally from other parts of Canada and thus used to the type of winter Ottawa presents. In fact, in 1984, at a time when I was out of work and dead broke I was offered a safe Conservative seat, Capilano, and answered thusly, "If you assure me that the Tories win and I lose, so that I will get all the perks of a losing candidate in a winning cause, I'm your man. But I'll surely win and there's no way I'll live in Ottawa, even for a day."

There is another factor. Like all converts, newcomers to British Columbia tend to become more passionate West Coasters than those born here. And the most passionate British Columbian of them all (even more than Duff Pattullo who came from Ontario and fought his fellow Liberals in Ottawa with a passion during the 1920s and 1930s) was William Andrew Cecil Bennett, who was born in New Brunswick.

The Socred years in British Columbia politics began when the spotlight first shone on W. A. C. Bennett following his surprise victory in the 1952 election. The coming to power of Mr. Bennett in 1952 was nothing short of a political miracle that demonstrated again, if it needed demonstrating, that timing is everything. A disgruntled Tory backbencher in the Coalition government of Conservatives and Liberals (formed in 1941, ostensibly as a patriotic gesture towards the war effort, in fact as a successful move to keep the socialist CCF out of power), Bennett crossed the floor in 1951 to sit as an independent, later joining the Social Credit Party. He was joined by Tilly Rolston, another disgruntled Tory MLA, an early supporter of Bennett's and the first woman in Canada to hold a cabinet portfolio. As the Coalition self-destructed, Bennett co-opted a loony-tunes organization called the Social Credit League of British Columbia and rode it to a narrow 19-18 victory over the CCF in the 1952 election. The Coalition dissolved and its component parts had very limited impact in their own right until Gordon Wilson in 1991, with a surprise election reminiscent of W. A. C. Bennett's in 1952, took the Liberals from no seats to Official Opposition. However, the Coalition did rise again, in another form. The CCF, in Opposition from 1933 to 1960, was reborn in 1961 as the NDP, which continued as Official Opposition until 1972, when Dave Barrett led the NDP to its first B.C. election victory. The reaction of the right was almost instantaneous. There was a need to "unite the right" (sound familiar?) and in 1975 the old Social Credit Party, reorganized and renamed the B.C. Social Credit Party, with the help of three of the four sitting Liberals and one of the two Tories banded together to form a new coalition. It won the December 11 election (with a rookie MLA named Rafe Mair in tow), and formed the government. But I'm ahead of myself. Back to 1952 and the death of the Coalition.

There is a marvellous story about the aftermath of this watershed election. The Lieutenant Governor, Clarence Wallace, dithered interminably over offering Mr. Bennett the government. He really didn't want to do it if he could find a way out. It was scarcely that he wanted the CCF in but along with many of the British Columbia establishment (the Wallaces owned shipyards) he was puzzled and not a little concerned about this Social Credit bunch that had suddenly won an election. There was, you see, no little concern being expressed in the Union Club and the Vancouver Club. Were the Socreds really committed to Major Douglas's incomprehensible financial theories? Would they be like their namesakes in Alberta and try to close newspapers? Would Mr. Bennett, like Bible Bill Aberhardt in Alberta, be doing Sunday religious programs on the radio? Eventually Mr. Wallace called upon the federal Liberals for advice and was told to do what he thought was best. Meanwhile, CCF leader Harold Winch said that they should have a chance because of their experience in the legislature. Besides, Tom Uphill, the "Labour" member from Fernie and the longest-serving MLA in B.C. history, would surely support him, making it a 19-19 tie.

Unknown to Mr. Winch, though, Mr. Bennett had an ace up his sleeve: a letter from Mr. Uphill supporting him.

The W. A. C. Bennett era was one of British Columbia first, last and always. To Bennett, British Columbia was a goblet for Ottawa to drain. While he professed loyalty to the country, Bennett never, ever, allowed national interests to be put ahead of his own, which were British Columbian to the core.

If one looks back today, in Bennett's time the unspoken and perhaps not fully thought-out ambition of British Columbians was to elect to Victoria a government that would protect them from Ottawa. Ottawa was and is seen by many British Columbians in the same way as the tenth-century Anglo-Saxons saw the Danes—as marauders to be paid off periodically with a Danegeld in the hope they would turn their attention elsewhere. As Rudyard Kipling said, however, "If once you have paid him the Danegeld, you never get rid of the Dane." And so it is with British Columbia and the federal government.

Probably the best example of B.C.'s independent spirit came with the Columbia River Treaty signed in 1964 between Canada and the United States. It was necessary to implement Bennett's "two rivers policy" of hydroelectric development. This treaty, though negotiated by the federal government, on B.C.'s behalf, with the United States was clearly done so on Bennett's terms. Lester Pearson, when he signed the treaty, said "I may be prime minister of Canada but Bennett is master of all he surveys."

W. A. C. Bennett was re-elected six times and served as premier for twenty years, during which he embarked on an ambitious program of public works and resource development. Throughout Bennett's tenure there was another dynamic at play—the struggle between left and right. More than any other province, British Columbia inherited the British trade union movement, complete with the British notion of class struggle, along with a healthy dose of far left unionism from the United States as exemplified by the International Workers of the World or the "Wobblies." The Wobblies started in Chicago in 1905 and used songs to fan the flames of discontent among workers.

The W. A. C. Bennett years were punctuated by a labour unrest made all the more troublesome by the need to repeatedly go to court. There being no Labour Relations Board to refer disputes to, the standard practice was for the union to commit some act the employer didn't like with the employer and his lawyers seeking an injunction from judges that were scarcely temperamentally inclined towards Organized Labour. The unhappy climax of this came in 1972 when then Labour Minister, Cyril Shelford, who ironically was inclined to be sympathetic to labour, was badly injured in a scuffle.

In 1972, when W. A. C. Bennett was soundly thrashed by the brash New Democrat Dave Barrett, British Columbia was a province generally united in its dislike of all things eastern but divided socially and politically in a big way.

This election left the Socreds with only ten seats and, as usually happens with a big upset, without their big guns. "Flying Phil" Gaglardi, the controversial Highways Minister, Health Minister Wes Black and Forests Minister Ray Williston were just some of the Socred front bench casualties. When W. A. C. Bennett, after a long vacation, decided in 1973 to retire and resign his seat, not many would have given the Socreds much of a chance to come back—especially as they were seen as not really a proper political party anyway. When Bennett's younger son, Bill, succeeded him in 1973 it seemed for all the world that the Socreds had become a political joke.

The Dave Barrett government brought in many long overdue reforms. In 1972 the NDP introduced social programs to fill the gaps the Socreds had left. They brought in reforms to the legislature such as a written *Hansard* for all house and committee proceedings and a question period. They brought in legislation to protect farmland from development, new public corporations such as the Insurance Corporation of British Columbia and a controversial royalty on mineral exploration. The NDP were destined to serve as a one-term government, not least because they were successfully portrayed by W. A. C. Bennett's younger son and successor Bill, as fiscal wastrels. In a clever, if somewhat disingenuous move, the Socreds played havoc with an NDP rule introduced to restrict debates on ministers' estimates to 135 hours, not an unreasonable restriction. The Socreds deliberately ran out the 135 hours before the Minister of Finance's estimates were tabled so that the Speaker had no option but to pass each vote without debate whereupon Bill Bennett toured the province calling down the heavens on the fiscally inept NDP with the slogan, "Not a dime without debate." The NDP, intemperately and foolishly, passed a motion to dock Mr Bennett's legislative pay while he was absent, making him not only an agitator but a martyr to fiscal responsibility as well.

In 1975, when the NDP lost to Bill Bennett, I became a member of his cabinet. As we went into the budget process it occurred to us that perhaps the time limits on the debate of ministerial estimates had not been such a bad idea after all. "You've got to be kidding" was the mildest of the retorts from the NDP when this was suggested and we went into debating estimates from March for much of that session, which didn't end until just before Christmas. In politics, as in real life, what goes around, comes around. In politics it usually happens faster.

I would argue that the NDP were doomed from the start. They were a provincial wing of a federal party and this was anathema to the core of British Columbia voters. This didn't come to the fore during the Barrett years, at least not in any tangible form. But in 1975, Bill Bennett and his deputy premier Grace McCarthy were able to reconstruct the old Social Credit League into the British Columbia Social Credit Party—a distinct B.C.–only entity with no connections of any sort outside British Columbia's borders. It became, for the most part, what the old Coalition had been except that there still were remnants of the Liberals and Tories, each of which had one member in the House after the 1975 election.

When Bennett and McCarthy were able to convince almost the entire non-socialist element of the voting public to join and support this coalition, Barrett was slaughtered. The proof of the success of the new coalition was that only two outsiders were elected in the December 1975 election: Gordon Gibson, a Liberal, and Dr. Scott Wallace, a Tory. Both of them were elected mostly on their immense personal popularity.

But the success of the Socreds in 1975 wasn't as simple as Bennett and McCarthy creating a British Columbia-only, non-left coalition. They badly needed credibility. The Socreds had been thrashed politically in 1972 and demoralized. Most of their big guns, as happens in political wipeouts, had been defeated. They were left with ten undistinguished MLAs led by "Daddy's boy," Bill Bennett.

Bill Bennett turned out to be not only a good premier but also a vicious alley fighter in the legislature (which was not called the "zoo" for nothing). Early on, a senior NDP cabinet minister hurled the "Daddy's Boy" insult across the house. Bennett met the barb with the rejoinder, "At least I know who my father was." His tormentor was a foundling.

On another occasion, Frank Howard, a tough bird who had been a long-time CCF-NDP MP before going into the B.C. legislature, taunted Bill Bennett about his record. "I'll match my record against yours any day," said Bennett to Howard who, when a youth, had done time for robbery. Bennett was not to be fooled with.

The gaining of public credibility by the new Socreds under Bill Bennett came in several ways. To start with, most of the province was fed up with the Barrett government which, if nothing else, had moved too fast and had shown too keen a dislike for business, especially the mining business. But that wasn't enough. Both the Tories and the Liberals claimed that they could govern better. In 1972, the presence of three parties in the race split the vote and elected the NDP, who held less than 40 percent of the popular vote.

The post-1972 "non left" was in turmoil. By dint of a number of events, including the Majority Movement for Freedom and Enterprise, an attempt to create a single, anti-socialist party, and the crossing of several prominent Liberals and Tories to the Socreds, the Social Credit Party unified behind Bill Bennett.

The media, led by Allan Fotheringham, a long-time Liberal supporter, dumped all over the new coalition. Calling it the "United Vegetable Party," they ensured the Socreds lots of publicity. They got all the support that comes from those who read what sneering columnists suggest they do and promptly do the opposite.

Under the party presidency of Grace McCarthy, the Socreds made another brilliant move in 1975. Recognizing that she was in a numbers game, and that parties don't survive on membership fees, McCarthy offered three-year memberships to the Social Credit Party for five dollars. Fotheringham had great fun with this and the membership grew by leaps and bounds with each of his derisory columns. Mrs. McCarthy knew that a huge, broad-based party would have a substantial impact. More than that, she realized that politics was about all that British Columbians were talking about. The more Socred memberships in the wallets and purses of the province, the better.

The new entity—and the British Columbia Social Credit Party was that—accomplished two things. First, it created a tent under which virtually all voters opposed to the NDP could feel comfortable and, second, it was a made-in-B.C. party through and through. From 1975 on, Social Credit was again a powerful political force, as the next four elections were to prove.

There was a third factor, however. Never gregarious, always serious if not severe looking, Bill Bennett began to get grudging respect, if not affection—Bill never got that until after he retired. Bill Bennett spoke in every hamlet in the province and people took to him as a man of competence, a sharp contrast to the image they had of Dave Barrett.

On December 11, 1975, the Socreds returned to power. The NDP, who curiously had virtually the same percentage of the popular vote in losing as they did in winning three and one-third years before, were out with Barrett losing even his own seat. Fast forward to November 1991. The Socreds are all but wiped off the map, with the Liberals under Gordon Wilson coming a surprising second and forming the official Opposition. By the next election the Socreds were member-less and they weren't even on the political radar screen. What had happened?

Bill Bennett won in 1975, again in 1979 and once more in 1983. He provided good government that showed a commendable social conscience. He had weathered mighty storms such as doubling government car insurance rates in one fell swoop and the recession of the early 1980s, which produced a public spending "restraint" program that saw, in July 1983, one of the largest political demonstrations in B.C. history. Labour unrest at this time bordered on the dangerous such that Jack Munro, president of the IWA for Canada, had to remind his own supporters that laws and policies were changed in the legislature, not in the streets. Indeed, with teachers and public employees on strike by November 1983 and a general strike threatened, Munro met in Kelowna with the premier and the general strike was called off. In return, Bennett introduced his program of fiscal restraint with only minor concessions. By 1986 Bennett had successfully launched Expo 86 and one might have thought that things for the Socreds looked pretty rosy.

But they weren't. The polls told Bennett that he would lose the next election. He had accomplished what he wanted accomplish, and in May 1986, Bennett announced a leadership convention for July.

The announcement of Bill Bennett's retirement came as a considerable shock to most British Columbians and exposed one glaring weakness in the Social Credit Party. Just as his father had not prepared a successor, neither had Bill. Indeed, Bennett's favourite, if he had one, seemed to be Bud Smith, a Kamloops lawyer who, while an acknowledged backroom genius, had never been elected. The race was wide open.

As one might expect, leadership that promised the premier's chair as an immediate reward drew all sorts of candidates. By the time of the convention, however, it was clear that one of four people would win. Bud Smith, with Ontario guru and veteran political organizer John Laschinger as his manager, had done much better in gaining delegates than most thought he would. Grace McCarthy, the grande dame of the party, had much support from caucus and the membership at large. Brian Smith, who like Bennett was a dour looking man but privately was very funny, was an unknown factor. And there was the populist of all populists, Bill Vander Zalm, out of the government since 1983, but very much a factor in the run for delegates.

Not for the first or the last time the Socred leadership race had the media fooled. They saw the two Smiths as the "Smith Brothers" and thought they had a deal to transfer support if one of them were knocked out of the race. They thought the same about McCarthy and Vander Zalm. They were very wrong as events would prove. Vander Zalm won the Socred leadership and the premier's job in a bitter fight that revealed no alliances whatever—indeed quite the opposite.

Bill Vander Zalm was and is an extraordinary man. A person of enormous personal charm and a devoted family man, he was mayor of Surrey from 1969 to 1975, as well as a minister in the Bill Bennett government from 1975 to 1983. Vander Zalm was nevertheless opposed for leadership by all but one of his former colleagues. (The lone supporter was Jack Davis, a brilliant but strange man whom Bill Bennett fired from cabinet in 1978 after Davis was caught in an expenses scandal that led to his conviction for theft.) Why was Vander Zalm, so popular with the masses, such an anathema to his colleagues?

Vander Zalm had some serious drawbacks. A hugely successful businessman, he had made his way to Canada after a desperate childhood in Nazi-occupied Holland, often forced to eat tulip bulbs while his father was, ironically, trapped in British Columbia when the Germans invaded. Vander Zalm had no formal education beyond high school. He compensated with a heavy use of personal charm and charisma. Vander Zalm's colleagues saw him as shallow and a man who not only couldn't form a consensus, but who viscerally opposed such things. He was stubborn to an enormous fault and utterly inflexible. His colleagues to a person liked, even loved Bill Vander Zalm but they saw him as less than competent as a minister and utterly lacking in the virtues needed to keep disparate points of view together in one government.

I covered the 1986 Whistler leadership convention for CKNW and also reported to the CBC with Bill Good, who was then hosting CBC's political coverage and is now a colleague at CKNW. The day before the vote Bill Good asked me, on air, what would happen if Bill Vander Zalm was selected as leader. "In two years," I replied, "he will have ruined the Social Credit Party." And so it proved.

The turning point in the leadership race came on the eve of the vote when BCTV and the Vancouver *Province* showed polls indicating that a Vander Zalm–led Social Credit Party could beat the NDP in the next election and that none of the others could. This became the only conversation on election eve and the following day the delegates, snatching victory from the jaws of a Bennett defeat, made Bill Vander Zalm the third leader of the Social Credit Party and B.C.'s premier.

Things went well for the new premier until the 1986 election. Vander Zalm's cabinet seemed content. So did the public. But he had made a strategic error, which, he was to tell me later, publicly on my show just before the 2001 provincial election, was the biggest mistake of his career. After the first ballot, when the two Smiths, McCarthy and Vander Zalm (with the most votes but far short of a majority) remained to go into the next round, Bud Smith, to the shock, nay horror, of many, crossed the floor to Vander Zalm. It was assumed that Smith and Vander Zalm had struck a deal by which Smith would be rewarded for crossing the floor, but that simply wasn't so. As he admitted later,

Vander Zalm should have included Smith in his cabinet not only to satisfy Lyndon Johnson's dictum about appointing J. Edgar Hoover to head the FBI, namely that it would have been better having him inside the tent pissing out than outside pissing in. There was a better reason—Bud Smith should have been in cabinet because Vander Zalm badly needed the advice and help the very wise young Mr. Smith could provide, a fact Vander Zalm candidly confessed to me.

At the time, the fall 1986 election looked as a near landslide by the popular hero over the inept NDP leader Bob Skelly. But there is more to it than that. Vander Zalm had started with an enormous lead over a Mr. Skelly, who stumbled out of the gate. But seasoned observers all agreed that if the campaign had been two weeks longer, then the result would have been very close indeed. For Vander Zalm had shown during the campaign what his old colleagues all knew—he didn't wear well. In the early going when Vander Zalm's charisma seemed to carry the day, all was well. As the campaign wore on, it was evident that the hard "right" positions he had taken back in 1975 when he told those on welfare he would find them shovels and put them to work, still guided his political philosophy. After the election, the Vander Zalm government began to unravel. Grace McCarthy and Brian Smith, both of whom he made cabinet ministers, resigned in 1988 over different issues, but issues nevertheless which pointed to a huge dissatisfaction with Vander Zalm as leader. Uncompromising at all times, Vander Zalm's "my way or the highway" approach forced five backbenchers to resign from caucus. For the very reasons his old colleagues, including me, foresaw, the Vander Zalm government crumbled. He simply could not lead, seeing every issue from the picky to the serious as a matter of principle on which to take an unshakeable stand. What would have been ordinary, garden variety scandals, such as a pub licence for a political pal, became major issues. By 1988— two years after Vander Zalm had become leader—the Social Credit Party had been shattered.

Could Humpy Dumpty be put back together again? The annual party convention in Penticton that fall proved that it could not be.

The issue in Penticton in 1988 was a leadership review and whether or not it should be by secret ballot. I remember Bill Bennett remarking to me over a drink on the eve of the convention that a party that denied democracy to its members couldn't survive. (I don't think Bennett was right—look at the federal Liberals—but he knew the Social Credit Party intimately.) The issue of how the ballot should be conducted was a public vote and old Socreds, such as the loquacious Phil Gaglardi and Don Phillips, the man known as "leather lungs," literally shouted down the opposition to Vander Zalm. The leader stayed—and the party remained broken—in fact now in much worse shape than before.

Things went from bad to worse. In 1990 Premier Bill Vander Zalm used Government House to entertain a shady Filipino businessman who wanted to buy Fantasy Gardens, the Richmond theme park that Vander Zalm had owned since 1984. The situation developed to the point that conflicts between the premier's private interests and public duty were obvious to all but him. He was so sure there was no problem he asked the highly respected former Saskatchewan Supreme Court Judge, Ted Hughes, to investigate and report. Vander Zalm thus violated the oldest of political rules, namely that you never order an investigation unless you know what the result will be. In March 1991 Mr. Hughes found the premier in conflict in several areas and the premier resigned.

Now the stage was set. It was not the survival of the premier that was at stake but whether or not the Social Credit Party, started by W. A. C. Bennett and made into a formidable force by Bill Bennett, would survive. From March 1991, when Vander Zalm resigned, the mass political suicide began.

Vander Zalm resigned immediately after Ted Hughes' finding, leaving an interim period before the leadership convention. Who were the Socreds going to make premier during this interim period? The decision was that of caucus and they had two choices. If they wanted to ensure that no one had any unfair advantage going into that convention, they could choose an interim caretaker premier with no leadership ambitions. Or they could choose Rita Johnston, who was the caucus favourite and who made no bones about the fact that she wanted the premier's job permanently. Russ Fraser, the non-lawyer Attorney General for a time, told caucus that if he were made premier, he would not seek the job at the convention. Allan Williams, who with other Liberals Pat McGeer and Garde Gardom had crossed the floor to join Bill Bennett in 1975 and was a highly regarded former Attorney General, told the caucus what may be the only bad advice he has ever given: that they shouldn't select anyone on an interim basis. For whatever reason remains a mystery. Perhaps Mr. Williams was simply a fan of Mrs. Johnston. He did support her at the convention and I still see, in my mind's eye, the ridiculous spectacle of the usually very dignified Allan Williams, QC, bedecked in "for Johnston" regalia, dancing in a conga line on the convention floor. The caucus made what was to be a fatal mistake of rejecting Mr. Fraser's offer and selected Rita Johnston as premier.

Rita Johnston is a fine woman and had been a reasonably able cabinet minister in the mostly inadequate Vander Zalm government. She was a legitimate contender. But she represented, whether she liked it or not, the right wing of the party. In the minds of the public, fairly or unfairly, she was a Vander Zalm acolyte. If she were the party leader going into the next election, she would wear this big time.

Grace McCarthy had been out of cabinet for three years, toiling away as a backbencher and making it clear in many ways that she deeply disapproved of the way the party was headed. I don't think anyone thought that Grace McCarthy, as leader of the Social Credit Party, could win the next election but virtually everyone knew that she would make it a race. They knew that the party, even if she led it to defeat, would be in a strong opposition position.

But Ms. Johnston went into the convention with a couple of things going for her. This was a Social Credit Party affair that had no public involvement and she was seen within the party as a loyal soldier who had stayed the course despite enormous difficulties. She had taken over when the government was at its nadir. Moreover, there was a strong anti-Grace section more in the caucus than in the party. Grace, for all her many charms, had been around long enough to make enemies. Those who had, like Johnston, stayed the course, resented the fact that Mrs. McCarthy had fled to a safe perch when she resigned early in 1988. To make matters worse, Grace dithered. First she wouldn't go in and then maybe she would; finally it was, "Well, if you really think I should, I guess I will." She called in all her political counters but it was too late—some had now been pledged to Mrs. Johnston. She left it too long and she was beaten.

After the vote, you could see the party split before your eyes. I covered the convention for BCTV, operating out of the mezzanine in the Convention Centre at Canada Place looking down on the delegates. And the rift was obvious. About half would go with Mrs. Johnston, on the bridge of the Titanic, and the rest would join the Liberal Party.

The Liberal Party? How did they get into the act?

The Liberal Party in British Columbia was in tatters after the Liberal triumvirate (McGeer, Williams and Gardom) crossed the floor in 1975. The estimable Gordon Gibson, after personally winning his seat in 1975, was a one-man band and he resigned a couple of years later. Without a seat, the Liberals stumbled from one unknown and unknowable leader to another until in the late 1980s a young college instructor named Gordon Wilson came on the scene. In 1987 Wilson became leader of the B.C. Liberals.

Wilson recognized that one of the problems with his party was that it was connected by umbilical cord to the federal Liberals. Wilson, a native British Columbian, knew how other British Columbians despised Ottawa, particularly the federal

Liberals. He proposed and got a divorce: the B.C. wing of the Liberal Party became the British Columbia Liberal Party. (That it was a divorce with bedroom privileges was obvious to many but under Wilson, there appeared to be an independent Liberal Party.)

Gordon Wilson, once in charge, took a strong public stance for British Columbia as he vigorously opposed the Meech Lake Accord, which Vander Zalm had supported. Without the collapse of the Social Credit Party, Mr. Wilson would simply have remained a political asterisk as one of many who led a party that traditionally finished down the list with the Western Canada Concept and the Rhinoceros Party in B.C. elections. But by the time Rita Johnston called the election in the fall of 1991, Wilson and the Liberals found themselves in a position to fill the vacuum the Socreds were about to leave. And that's exactly what happened. Wilson found himself head of the second largest party in the legislature and the leader of Her Majesty's Loyal Opposition to the NDP. The Social Credit Party was left with seven seats. The Socreds were dead or at least terminally ill.

The story of the Liberal Party in British Columbia and the ongoing saga of B.C. politics in general doesn't end there. After a personal scandal that saw Gordon Wilson virtually tossed out of the Liberal leadership in 1993, he formed a party of his own, the Progressive Democratic Alliance, which consisted mainly of himself and his stunningly beautiful and talented wife, Judi Tyabji. There he languished until early 1999 when, having lost his seatmate, he decided to cross the floor to the NDP and take on a cabinet position as Minister of Aboriginal Affairs. This decision was as calamitous an event for the middle of the road voter as had been Mrs. Johnston's decision to become interim premier or Grace McCarthy's dithering. Without the Progressive Democratic Alliance as a voting alternative, the middle of the road was left again to the Liberal Party.

By 2001, the NDP had managed in ten years in government to become (second only to Brian Mulroney's national Tories) the most despised governing party in history. Everyone but the hard left had deserted them. At the same time, the Gordon Campbell Liberals were not so much popular for their leader or their policies, but because they weren't the NDP. To a great many British Columbians, including me, they were still Liberals and that was enough to be highly suspicious of them. But by May 2001 they could have, as the great mayor of New York Fiorello La Guardia once said, "run on a laundry ticket" and beaten the NDP.

Stand back and take a look at the May 2001 election as though Gordon Wilson had stayed the course as leader of the Progressive Democratic Alliance and had run a full or near full slate of candidates. Surely there would have been a repeat of his success as a Liberal in 1991 and he again would have been leader of the Opposition. The Liberals would have won, but heading the middle of the road Progressive Democratic Alliance, strictly a made-in-British Columbia party, would have been Gordon Wilson in the perfect position to pick up those who were mad at the NDP but unwilling to support the Liberals. Then Wilson could have waited, with bated breath, for Liberal backbenchers, upset as backbenchers always are, to fall like ripe plums into his lap.

But other events intervened and the play continues. Gordon Campbell's Liberal government will become unpopular—perhaps hugely so. There are almost certain to be defections from their large caucus. As they work more and more with the federal Liberals, the old B.C. resentments will fester.

Someone has to stand in Opposition to the government. Can the NDP come back? Highly unlikely. What about the Socreds? They're stone cold dead in the marketplace.

What the province will crave is another disgruntled backbencher such as W. A. C. Bennett crossing the floor and co-opting a political vehicle. Will we see a reprise of the miracle performed in similar circumstances by Bill Bennett and Grace McCarthy, working together to resurrect a political party? Who will fill the vacuum left by the all but vanished NDP? What form will they take? That remains to be seen. But, in the immortal words of former Socred MLA and cabinet minister Don Phillips, "The leopard never changes its stripes." British Columbians, I would argue now more than ever, do not like national parties operating their government in Victoria. I don't think the NDP can make up sufficient ground to challenge in the 2005 election. Yet, surely the Campbell government will have lost much of its support by then if only because nurses, health workers and doctors all have their contracts up for negotiation at that time, creating a political vacuum in the centre and on the left.

Let me go out on a limb and predict that some Liberal back-benchers will break away and if—a big word—one of them has some political presence, the vacuum will be filled by a party yet to be named.

THE BILL BENNETT
NO ONE KNEW

L et me lay out before you my bias. With the possible exception of his father, William Richards "Bill" Bennett was the
best premier British Columbia ever had. So there.

It is not my intention to prove that rather overwhelming statement but to tell you about the Bill Bennett I knew as one of the
members of his very first cabinet, sworn in December 22, 1975.

In order to understand why I admire Bill so much, a bit of
history and context is required. The Bill Bennett years, from
1973 to 1986, were a time of considerable political turmoil in
British Columbia. The NDP, elected in August 1972, defeated
Bill's father, W. A. C. Bennett, who had reigned as premier for
twenty years and had become unpopular almost the instant they
were elected. Unfortunately the opponents of the NDP were
divided into three parties—Liberals, Conservatives and Socreds,
each of whom devoutly believed that they and they alone could
defeat Dave Barrett. (When Barrett called a surprise election for
December 11, 1975, he caught even his own party off-guard and
ill-prepared.) Like many politically active—and ambitious—
people opposed to the NDP, I was pondering where I should
park my support. Indeed, in my case, I was pondering where I
would try to get nominated.

I first met Bill in 1974 shortly after he had won a by-election
for the South Okanagan seat which his father, W. A. C. Bennett,
had retired from a few months before. We met in Kamloops at a
cattle sale and I was impressed by Bill's determination. In fact I
don't think before or since I have met a man with such a steely
gaze of absolute determination to win.

At the time I was an alderman on the Kamloops City Council and was pondering a political future. I had met a couple of times with Derril Warren, the Conservative leader, and was considering running for office under that banner. Around this time Jarl Whist, my former law partner and a staunch Liberal, had formed a one-man band, which he called Stamp Out Socialism. But SOS had foundered, with Whist being called a "jackboot." (Little did his critics know that Whist was not German but a Norwegian Canadian who had spent the war under the Nazi heel.) One Sunday Jarl called me and several others to his home to discuss what could be done to get rid of the NDP—he had concluded that the Liberals weren't going to do it. We decided to form a movement called The Majority Movement for Freedom and Private Enterprise. The idea was that such a province-wide movement would bless candidates who could beat the NDP and negate the vote splitting that had enabled them to gain power in the first place. The manifesto was signed (as Casey Stengel used to say, "You could look it up") by Jarl Whist and Rafe Mair.

An amazing thing happened. Support for the Majority Movement spread like wild fire. The next thing we knew, the Vancouver lawyers including Arnold Hean and John Macdonald had all but taken it over and it was soon embraced by prominent political personages in Victoria including then-alderman and prominent lawyer Ian Stewart. Just as quickly the movement petered out, but it left in its wake the strong sense that we all had to unite behind someone. That someone turned out to be Bill Bennett.

Also in late 1973 a by-election was called in North Vancouver following the resignation of Liberal MLA Dave Brousson. Liberal Gordon Gibson won this by-election but the Socreds came within fifty odd votes of winning. This was a near miracle considering how the Socreds had been thrashed in 1972 and was largely due to the efforts of Grace McCarthy who, defeated herself in 1972, saw Bill Bennett for what he was—a remarkably determined young man dedicated to rebuilding the party around him.

This by-election near-win galvanized the so-called "right." In no particular order Derril Warren quit as Tory leader, Tory MLA Hugh Curtis crossed the floor to join the Socreds, followed in 1975 by three Liberals: Pat McGeer, Allan Williams and finally Garde Gardom. (McGeer's move was especially helpful. Born into a Liberal dynasty—his uncle Gerry had been Vancouver's colourful mayor from 1934–1936 and again in 1946 and 1947, a Liberal MP and a Senator—Pat McGeer was the provincial Liberal Party leader from 1968–1972 and his defection gave huge credibility to the reviving Socreds.)

But it wasn't only elected MLAs who were important. For the Socreds to gain credibility they needed active members of other parties and in 1975 they netted the quintessential Tory in British Columbia, Peter Hyndman, who had run against the Socreds in 1972 and again in the North Vancouver by-election as a Conservative. The remarkable Socred convention held in 1975 at the Hyatt Regency was stacked to the rafters with people who, like me, had never cast a vote for Social Credit in their lives. (My first Socred vote was for myself later that year.) The people of the province, especially the pundits, were all watching. The decision was taken by Bill Bennett and Grace McCarthy that there would be a new party, the British Columbia Social Credit Party, which would replace the old Social Credit League and that the doors would open wide to everyone who wasn't a supporter of the NDP.

Part of the deal was that the Social Credit Party could, if the delegates wished, change the name of the party so as to better bind the wounds of Tories and Liberals who had fought so hard against the old Socreds. When the matter was debated, behind me at the microphone on the convention floor was Peter Hyndman. I asked him what his position was going to be, fully expecting him of all people to say that he wanted to have a new party name that had friendlier connotations for all the former enemies coming into the tent. Hyndman mumbled a few platitudes and I saw it was my turn. I spoke in favour of changing the party name. Hyndman, the bitter enemy of the Socreds, was next. I could scarcely believe my ears! "Why," he intoned, "the Social Credit name was a fine old name and embodied all the very best in British Columbia politics and government, blah, blah, blah ...." It was a considerable lesson in politics for a neophyte named Mair. The Social Credit Party was back, with Bill Bennett at the helm.

All this brings me to my first point that not only was Bill Bennett a very determined man, he had brains to go with that determination. Never a great public speaker (he was better than his father but that's faint praise indeed), he could nevertheless rally the troops. Moreover, somehow he had to relegate old Socreds such as Phil Gaglardi (who for all his peccadilloes had a strong following) to a respectable place in the ashcan. Bill Bennett managed it all with consummate skill, despite the biting sarcasm and cynicism of the press, especially Allan Fotheringham and Jack Webster. Being his father's son was far from an advantage—it simply brought sneers from many and disbelief from others. In less than two years Bill Bennett had restored the B.C. Social Credit Party to a position from which it could compete successfully.

After my initial meeting with Bill Bennett in Kamloops in 1974, I went to Victoria to meet with him more formally. The legislature was in session and I watched as Bennett orchestrated the fight against Premier Dave Barrett and his government. I was impressed. I met with him over a drink and can remember only two things—no cabinet post was guaranteed anyone, and he seemed utterly without humour.

In 1975 Bill Bennett and Grace McCarthy pulled off one of the great upset, comeback elections in B.C. history and the Socreds won a landslide victory. For me it meant enormous change—no longer was I a small-town lawyer in Kamloops but a cabinet minister. To be truthful I was scared as hell. I remember feeling my legs shake so badly as I was sworn in and that I hoped no one would notice. (My wife Eve did!)

I particularly remember our first cabinet meeting the day we were sworn in at which then Deputy Provincial Secretary Laurie

Wallace told the premier that his father always had his Attorney General sit to his right. "Garde," said Bennett to his new Attorney General, looking Wallace straight in the eye, "you will sit on my left." Bill Bennett knew that after his father, he had a lot of trees to pee on and he was going to get 'em all quickly.

For a year I was scared stiff of Bill Bennett. He was so severe and evidently so humourless that I never knew quite where I stood. It took a year before Bennett felt secure enough to loosen up. You can understand why. His senior cabinet ministers—Pat McGeer, Allan Williams and Garde Gardom—were very power-ful former enemies of his father. Grace McCarthy, scarcely an enemy but never known as close to Bennett, had enormous clout with the party she was seen as single-handedly taking from polit-ical oblivion to victory. He had two cabinet ministers who had run against him for the leadership in 1973. And he had raw rook-ies such as Jim Nielsen, Tom Waterland and me. Making this diverse group into a team took some doing. But Bennett did it.

The first year was rough. Right off the bat we were faced with bailing out the Insurance Corporation of British Columbia, which the NDP had founded in 1973 and had managed to run $180 million or thereabouts in the red in less than two years. This stinging nettle had to be grasped and rates had to be sub-stantially increased at a corporation many Socred supporters wanted disbanded. There was enormous pressure on all of us but, not yet liking the man, we respected Bennett's leadership and stuck it out.

The legislative session that began on March 17, 1976, was brutal. The NDP had convinced themselves that they had been cheated out of victory that past December and made the session what must surely have been the most unpleasant in British Columbia's history. In fact, they started before the session opened. Speaker-elect Ed Smith had allocated office space to the NDP which they didn't agree with so, contrary to invariable practice at that time, they opposed Smith's election as speaker, putting forth as their candidate their former Attorney General

Alex Macdonald. This process, completed with raucous shouting matches, all in front of the dignitaries assembled in the chamber, kept the Lieutenant Governor Walter Owen (who was to formally open the session) cooling his heels outside for an hour. From there it was all downhill. While testing our loyalty, these events galvanized the caucus behind Bill Bennett as leader. By the end of 1976 Bill Bennett had demonstrated to his cabinet, his caucus, his party and the public that he was in charge and that was that.

It was then we began to see the humorous side of Bennett. He had always been lightning quick with the retort but suddenly we saw that he was very funny indeed. It is always hard to remember individual cases of humour but I well remember accompanying Bennett to a western premier's conference. At that time we were all in awe of Alberta Premier Peter Lougheed, next to whom I was seated at dinner. Just as I was sipping from my glass of wine Bennett made a quip and I started to laugh so hard that wine shot out of my nostrils—just like milk used to when we were kids—all over my suit and the tablecloth. I was mortified but Bennett simply said, "Rafe is from Kamloops, you know, so he has a little trouble remembering just which orifice is used for wine."

Over the next few years I got to know Bill Bennett much better as a person. We travelled a lot together. I was responsible for constitutional affairs in which Bennett had a keen interest. We became friends—not close friends, but friends. I'm sure he had closer relations with other ministers yet, having said that, I think every one of us thought the others were in some mysterious "inner circle" from which we were excluded. In fact, I don't believe that there was an "inner circle."

As the years passed, the Bill Bennett cabinet became very comfortable with itself and its leader. There was always an atmosphere of potential humour. Hugh Curtis, a rather pompous person publicly, was a keen wit and he and Bennett often fed off each other. Allan Williams had a dry wit, Garde

Gardom had great bluffness and Jim Nielsen was a master of the one-liner. I'm not saying that I looked forward to cabinet meetings because they were loads of fun, but after the first year they were places where funny things could happen at any moment.

My association with the Bill Bennett cabinet ended in early January 1981. I had received and accepted what was then a stunning offer to go into radio. Although I thought I could do a political program and still serve as MLA, later that month it became obvious that I couldn't be both a critic of the government and part of its caucus. One practical problem was that the House sat in the mornings on Friday and because I was doing a morning broadcast, would always miss that sitting.

I phoned Bill at his Kelowna home in late December 1980 (I was Minister of Health at the time) and he seemed genuinely stunned and unhappy when I told him of my radio job offer. We arranged to meet at his office in a few days. When I arrived at the appointed hour Bill said, "Rafe, do you have a liquor cabinet in your office?" I replied that I did. "Does it have anything in it?" "Always." "Well," said Bennett, "as you know my Dad never drank so I have none here. What do you say we repair to your office?" We did, and we polished off a bottle of Scotch during a wonderful, though sad evening where, like a couple of old warriors parting, we reminisced, laughed and almost cried a bit, too.

It had been five years almost to the day since I had been taken into cabinet, knees-a-shaking. I had served under a man I more than respected but genuinely liked. I can say without fear of contradiction that with perhaps two exceptions—Jack Davis who was fired after being convicted for stealing and maybe Bill Vander Zalm—every one of Bill Bennett's ministers would have crawled a mile on their hands and knees over broken glass for the guy.

Bill Bennett was tough but he was fair. If you got into trouble, he stood up for you. If he had something to say to you, it was behind closed doors. He did tough, unpopular things and he expected you, once the decision had been taken, to support him. And he always got that support because you knew that however unpopular the policy might initially be, it was right.

There is another aspect of Bill Bennett the politician that the public doesn't understand. Every party has its left wing, its moderate wing and its right wing, within the context of the overall party philosophy, of course. I was on the left and so was Bill Bennett. During my years as Minister of Consumer and Corporate Affairs from November 1976 to November 1978 I put through more consumer legislation than anyone before or since. To give but one example, in a caucus that had six car dealers, two of whom were senior members of cabinet, in 1977 I pushed through the Motor Dealer's Licensing Act, which the car industry hated like poison. It could not have happened without the support of Bill Bennett. In the Ministry of Consumer and Corporate Affairs I fought 'em all—the bankers, the stockbrokers, the liquor interests, the lot—and Bennett supported me all the way.

In 1978, with the considerable help of my deputy, Tex Enemark, I made a change to the liquor laws which had a profound and lasting effect. Until then most of the wine grown in British Columbia was of the cheap "plonk" variety. Tex and I were convinced by our travels abroad and by talks with small farmers in the Interior that we could do better—much better—if we allowed the small winery to develop in the way it had in Europe and California. We developed a licence that permitted the "cottage" industry to develop. The success has been staggering as B.C. wines have now become world class, both in reds as well as whites. (We were told reds were out of the question because of the climate.)

There was considerable opposition from the established wineries, some of which were owned by large distilleries, and every imaginable reason was given as to why this was a terrible thing to do. But, with a very courageous Premier Bill Bennett behind us, the policy was adopted even though it was in Bennett's constituency that most of the big wineries plied their trade. Without question, says he unashamedly immodest, this move was the most substantial change in British Columbia agriculture since the arrival of the apple tree. (Indeed it was the problems of the fruit industry that made our policy possible.)

I have often said, tongue in cheek, that there ought to be a statue of Tex and me outside the city gates of Summerland but we'll have to be content to have this event recorded here.

One day, perhaps, the whole story will be written. When that happens perhaps the real story of the immense legal problems Bill got into in the early 1990s through his brother Russell and Herb Doman will be told. In the meantime this friend and colleague of William Richards "Bill" Bennett is here to tell you that he was a hell of a fine leader, an extremely witty companion, a good friend and a premier who looks very good indeed compared to those who followed him. He looks pretty damned good, period.

ON THE WORLD IN GENERAL

PROSPERITY OR DEATH?

Globalization has got everyone concerned but, more than anyone, it has the left in a flap. When I say "left" I mean the old-line socialists and labour leaders who sing from their tatty old songbook, leading off with "Solidarity Forever." They become apoplectic at the mention of the word. There is a great gnashing of teeth and wringing of hands as they predict with certainty that the sky is falling. The trouble is that while the socialist solution never did work, it is now so outdated that modern social democratic parties, such as are found in Europe, and New Labour in the United Kingdom don't even pay lip service to the old notions. "New Labour" in Britain is, in short, a "left" that has accepted much of capitalism and puts getting elected far, far ahead of any leftist philosophical positions of the past or the present. The "new" left as espoused by Naomi Klein and her acolytes are directly descended from the leftists of their parents' generation in the 1960s. Socialism died with communism in 1989 when the Berlin Wall came tumbling down. If socialistic principles couldn't work under compulsion, how could they work in democracy?

Ronald Reagan is credited in many circles with bringing down the old Soviet Union because he money-whipped them. He did drive the armaments race to new expensive heights that no doubt tipped the balance. But the real killer of socialism, whether of the forced or voluntary kind, was the consumer age's marriage to the communications age. I'll never forget a 1983 visit to China where, near the Hong Kong border, there were hundreds of television aerials pointed at stations in Hong Kong.

Authorities could really do nothing about it. And as the consumer goods and western way of life started to turn up on television screens in living rooms behind the Iron Curtain the difficulties facing communist governments there became insurmountable. It was a modern version of the old First World War song, "How're you going to keep 'em down on the farm, now that they've seen Paree?"

With the end of the Cold War and the rise of consumption and ease of communications, the pool of capital available started to look for places to invest. With the rise of the computer it was no longer possible for countries to pass serious currency restrictions because, with the push of a button, the money to be controlled was whisked off to a safer place. If a country did succeed in forcing unpopular restrictions on a pool of capital, other capital shunned it in future dealings. There is, of course, a myth based upon umpteen conspiracy theories that somewhere out there, some sinister person is controlling the world's capital and using it for wicked purposes. The fact is that capital, like filings to a magnet, is attracted to the best and safest deal. It will tolerate government interference to a degree because taxes can't be avoided but it will always go where there is the best bang for the buck.

The old left, never ready to let an old battle cry die down, talks of withdrawing from NAFTA and other sillier ideas. Even the new left, in moments of rationality, at least privately admits that the new world must be accommodated and appropriately changed, not abolished.

There are challenges, lots of them. Not everyone is a winner in the new global economy, not every country nor every person. In fact there are lots of losers. But the compensations have to come from sound government—and personal decisions—which recognize that the "electronic herd," as Tom Friedman calls the new pool of capital in his brilliant book *The Lexus and the Olive Tree: Understanding Globalization* (Farrar, Straus and Giroux, 2000). Capital can be eased about and directed with guidance, but it's not going to disappear.

The new world is here and just like the Industrial Revolution, it cannot be stopped, only accommodated and dealt with.

The "new" left moves around the western world looking for conferences to protest. Seattle, Washington, Quebec City and Genoa have seen how rowdy this left can become, lamentably, with a death in Genoa. It is interesting—and I would argue—unfortunate that the traditional parties of the left have not been able to accommodate the anti-globalization movement. They can't do so because this "new" left isn't new at all—it's the same youthful left that's always been there but never votes because basically it's anarchist and becomes three-piece suited conservative when it reaches age thirty-five.

The so-called "left" in Europe is so wrapped up in its own form of globalization called the European Union that it is on the other side of the fence from the "new" left. The Labour Party in Britain is now as conservative, if not more so, than were the Tories of John Major.

The new globalization can be acknowledged, because there is no other alternative, yet dramatically altered. This will require international cooperation and, frankly, the signs are not good. Probably the most obvious example is the Kyoto Accord, which the United States and, so far, Canada, refuse to ratify. An international commercial legal system is possible, but not probable in the near term. NAFTA was supposed to supply such a system within its boundaries but has failed for the same reason most legal systems fail: parties, through skilful lawyers, can adjourn until the aggrieved party is forced to make a bad settlement. Nothing, of course, is as important as finding ways to avoid war. Having said that, wise countries need to work out how to ride globalization as a vehicle to prosperity rather than as a hearse to the burial park.

Both options are presently open.

A "Major" Politician

I have long been an admirer of John Major, the last Conservative prime minister of the United Kingdom. After reading his book, *John Major: The Autobiography* (HarperCollins, 1999), my admiration, if anything, increased. For Mr. Major, unlike almost all who write their own story, confesses plenty of error, perhaps more than he needs to, and shows not a scintilla of bitterness. The book is still on the shelves in both hard and soft cover and for very good reason. Here is a politician who was not only honest to a fault but eminently likeable. To round out his attractiveness, he was damned unlucky.

Major's book has a special importance because the Major era marked the end of the Tories, probably for a very long time. It also marked the start of "New" Labour. When Britain is finally fully committed to the European Union, this era will be fascinating to study.

John Major is a remarkable man born of two circus performers and bears a name that was not his father's real name but a pseudonym. His father was sixty-five when Major was born but was a hero to Major, as was his mother, who had a merry old time forgiving her husband his many and frequent transgressions. The family was poor though not in abject poverty and young John was brought up in the part of London that customarily spawns devout Labour supporters.

Major cut his political teeth on Lambeth politics, representing the borough of Brixton. This down and dirty political experience clearly gave him not only his conservative approach but taught him never to take himself or politics too seriously.

Major's rise to the prime minister's job was meteoric. Elected to Parliament in the Thatcher victory in 1979 he became a parliamentary secretary in 1981, an assistant whip in 1983 and a minister (though not in cabinet) in 1986. Then in 1987 Major began an extraordinary three-year climb to the top of what Disraeli called the "greasy pole." In June 1987 he joined cabinet as Chief Secretary to the Treasury and went into cabinet becoming a Privy Councillor (entitling him to the title Right Honourable). In 1989 he became Foreign Secretary. Later that year he was Chancellor of the Exchequer and on November 27, 1990, he became prime minister. Major replaced Margaret Thatcher in a remarkable series of events that saw him help nominate Mrs. Thatcher after her leadership was challenged, only to find himself a couple of weeks later her successor. In April 1992, against all odds, Major won a general election with a majority of twenty-one.

Almost from the start Major's career as prime minister had problems and most of them had to do with the European Community. Neither the Tories nor Labour were unanimous on Britain's role in Europe but during the Major years the principal decisions came into focus. In a brilliant move Major gained an opt-out provision in the Maastricht Treaty so that Britain had a choice as to whether or not to join a common currency. Then, urged on by Labour, the business community and most of his own party, but still with reluctance, he joined Britain in the exchange rate mechanism, which required Britain to keep the value of the pound within certain prescribed limits. This turned out to be his Thermopylae. The bitterness between Norman Lamont, Major's Chancellor of the Exchequer, and Major still plays itself out in Tory politics.

On Black Wednesday, September 16, 1992, Britain was forced by the market, and at huge cost, to leave the exchange rate mechanism. From that moment on Major's administration was "snake bit."

During his entire term as prime minister John Major had to

fight the backbench of his party, who, in responding to Tory constituencies, chafed at further involvement in Europe. All this time, a similarly divided Labour caucus remained silent and out of the public spotlight. Moreover, Major was plagued with one scandal after another within his caucus and cabinet. Most were mild scandals involving sexual meanderings but the big one, "cash for questions," still has serious lingering effects within the Conservative Party. (Several backbenchers were subject to a "sting" operation by the *Sunday Times* who caught them taking large amounts of cash for tabling questions on behalf of "clients" in the House of Commons.)

Looking back at Major's prime ministership one has to concede that he was, for all these things, a good prime minister. He came to power during a recession with high inflation and high interest rates. He left office in 1997 with prosperity, low inflation and low interest rates. Major saw Britain through the Gulf War and re-established good relations with the United States, though, during a blip in 1992, Tory strategists helped the Republicans in that year's election, much annoying the Democrats under Bill Clinton.

John Major: The Autobiography is a long book at 735 pages but fascinating. It reads just as Mr. Major sounds. It is candid, fair and fascinating. Through it all one gleans the story of a talented, decent man, very lucky in his mate and family. But he was unlucky in his chosen profession, if you count coming from the east end of London to No. 10 Downing Street as unlucky.

THE CHANGING (MIS)FORTUNES
OF WAR

It is fifty-seven years since the detonation of an atomic bomb at Hiroshima, Japan, killing more than 75,000 people and the bombing, three days later, of Nagasaki, killing about 40,000 people. In fact, the death toll was much higher than that when those who died from the after-effects are counted. In a common grave in the Peace Park in Hiroshima 10,000 are buried.

The debate about the need to drop the bombs will continue. Many question the reason given that the bombs would end the war—so it was said and so it proved to be—and avoid the bloodbath that was certain to occur if an invasion of Japan was needed. They say Japan was already beaten. What is certain is that President Harry S. Truman showed no hesitation to use the atomic bomb and said that the decision never cost him a minute's sleep.

I'm not sure which side I support on this issue. I have visited Hiroshima, its Atomic Bomb Museum, its Peace Park and I've seen Atom Bomb Dome, the Meccano set–like remains of the only building left standing at ground zero. I've seen the shadow of a man etched on a piece of granite that was once the step of a bank where the man sat, waiting for the doors to open. I've reflected on the fact that Hiroshima was not a military target and that the most military thing about it was the nearby Allied prisoner-of-war camp. The bomb was dropped on a weekday in the middle of rush hour, a time certain to cause the maximum number of civilian deaths.

Yet, were even more lives saved because Japan surrendered a few days later? We're left with the unsettling thought that the lives the Allies were concerned about saving were the lives of white people, not the lives of the Japanese who were the "bad" guys during the war—the "slanty-eyed yellow bastards."

The only certainty is that we now know what happens when you use a nuclear weapon. Granted, these two bombs were like firecrackers compared to what exists today. The fact remains that the world has seen two nuclear weapons dropped in anger. If Hiroshima and Nagasaki did nothing else, they showed the world a taste of what nuclear war would look like and perhaps in this backhanded, macabre way, kept the world from blowing itself up.

The value of this knowledge has been enormous. During the Cold War we had the theory of mutually assured destruction (MAD), with practical evidence to back it up. Might we have had a nuclear war had such a demonstration of power not occurred? Who's to know? But we do have some historical experience to go on. In 1914 there was, with one exception, no indicator of what a modern war would be like. Before the "Great War," the last dust-up was the Franco-Prussian War of 1870—except for the Boer War, that is. The Boer War was different because it was mostly regular troops trying to deal with guerrillas. That war did have some unlearned lessons for the French and Americans, much later, in Vietnam. But the Franco-Prussian War, in which France was defeated and the allegiance of the southern German states won, was all but over after the battle at Sedan. The Crimean War with Turkey, Britain and France against Russia, more than a half a century before in 1853–1856, still involved, in the main, clashes on horseback.

The exception was the American Civil War, during which the Union States defeated a secession attempt by slave states. Because it didn't happen in Europe, where the lesson was most needed, it was ignored. One can only speculate what might have happened if the general staffs of Britain, France and Germany had studied the American Civil War and learned its obvious lessons about the effects of modern weapons, especially the machine gun, on troops in battle.

When war started following the assassination of Archduke Franz Ferdinand on June 28, 1914, it was assumed that it would all be over by Christmas. Crowds burst into the streets of London, Paris and Berlin cheering like mad in patriotic fervour. So out of touch with the realities of modern war was the general staff (and the public for that matter), it took more than five years for everyone to learn that machine guns kill people who leave the trenches.

Now, of course, one of the threats of nuclear war, the Soviet Union and America getting cross with one another, has gone. There is still the possibility of accident but that is greatly diminished. Now the threat comes not just from "rogue" states but from rogues themselves. Moreover, longstanding quarrels such as in the Middle East and in the Indian subcontinent have the real capacity to break into deliberately started nuclear wars. And the American Nuclear Shield plan of George W. Bush raises the notion that a perfect defence simply raises fear of a "first strike" from the nation under the shield. But as presidents Bush and Putin move their relationship forward it seems that this fear may be eliminated as well.

What is chilling, however, is that terrorists do not need to know nuclear secrets to strike with nuclear weapons. They only need the means of delivery, and that can be no more complicated than a smuggled suitcase.

How ironic it is that whereas for fifty-five years it was the peace-monger screaming at governments to get some sense in their heads—and they did—we now find that it is no longer the demented nation to be feared, but the demented individual.

POLITICAL MATURITY

Canada is a very immature country politically and I'm damned if I know why. We are rich in tradition and neighbours next to a country that, for all the asperity of its politics, still manages to call its past presidents "Mr. President" long after they have retired or been turfed from office. In November 2001 we saw President George W. Bush, a right-wing Republican, successfully mend fences with the American far left, the Kennedy family.

I have just finished reading the last of three volumes of letters and memoirs of Lady Violet Bonham Carter who died in 1969 after a lifetime in British politics as a Liberal—no mean task. She was the daughter of H. H. Asquith, the Liberal prime minister who was ousted in 1916 by his fellow Liberal, David Lloyd George. She was the mother of long-time Liberal and sometime MP Mark Bonham Carter and grandmother of the actress Helena Bonham Carter.

Her only book of consequence was the marvellous *Winston Churchill: An Intimate Portrait* (Harcourt Brace, 1965), which takes Churchill only until 1916 but is an absorbing account of the great man's early career. At an early dinner party Churchill turned to the then Miss Asquith and said "Violet, we are all worms but I do believe that I am a glow worm!" As it turned out to be.

Throughout Lady Bonham Carter's life she remained true to the Liberalism of her father as opposed to that of Lloyd George. I tell you this because it shows you that her politics were not only loyal but wrapped in bitterness. The split between her father and Lloyd George in 1916 split the Liberal Party forever and is still being played out now, nearly ninety years later. She despaired of Churchill returning to the Tories after having deserted them for the Liberals in 1905 and was no fan of the Labour Party. Yet her memoirs—for that's what these wonderful readable volumes are—are full of intimate social relations with men and women of all parties. To be sure, she does not like all her social contacts—Lord Beaverbrook was particularly forever on her shit list—but she had social and political relations with them all. She described men such as Attlee and Ernest Bevin, long her political foes, with great affection and dealt both harshly and gently with men like Macmillan and Sir Alec Douglas Home. Her love for Winston Churchill, laced with the occasional moment of despair for day-to-day antics, remains undiminished until the end of the great man's life. Whether or not she and Churchill were ever lovers in her youth is doubtful but there is no doubt that she bore a special love for him—and for his Liberal wife Clementine—her entire life.

Through it all, these men and women of different backgrounds and differing politics all worked, supped, drank and socialized with one another. All were modest enough to know that they had no right to assume, no matter how strong their views or how nasty the fight, that there weren't other legitimate points of view than their own.

I well remember when, in 1977 as Minister of Consumer and Corporate Affairs in the Bill Bennett government, I piloted a new Residential Tenancy Act through the B.C. legislature. Here was a long act bound to raise socialist hackles in many areas. My critic, the NDP veteran Norm Levy, and I cracked open a bottle of Scotch one evening and worked out how the bill could be handled. In no way did he compromise his New Democratic Party, nor did I mine. We simply agreed on a rough outline of how matters would proceed so he could advise those of his colleagues about what to say on the matter when they were called on to speak. This most difficult of bills passed the final two readings in one afternoon and one evening session.

When some of my caucus colleagues learned that I had actually broken bread with the hated NDP and made "deals," they were furious. Such was the way the Bill Bennett Socreds and the Dave Barrett New Democrats behaved with one another.

This feeling has continued unabated as the sons of Socred, the B.C. Liberals, refused to designate the two NDP members left after the May 2001 debacle as the Official Opposition. It was spite, longstanding spite.

Things, I'm told, aren't much better on the federal scene.

Canadian political animals of all political persuasions could do worse than read Lady Bonham Carter's memoirs. They might learn some perspective and perhaps even a bit of humility.

THE COLD WAR: AN ANALYSIS

Shortly after the tragedy of September 11, 2001, the "how-evers" began to come out of the woodwork. You know who I mean. People who say, "The events of September 11 were horrible, 'however'" followed by a litany of complaints against the United States. These people include Suneri Thobani, a University of British Columbia professor active in the women's movement, who made a speech shortly after September 11 in effect saying that the United States got what it deserved.

I was born in the Great Depression, grew up during the Second World War and spent my adult life in varying degrees of fear that my family and I would be consumed in a nuclear holocaust. I recall the Cuban Missile crisis of 1962 like it was yesterday. I had my wife and four little kids ready to run to the Interior of the province to avoid the nuking we knew was coming.

Now, all you "howevers," pay close attention. At the close of the Second World War the Cold War started. It was no less a war for all that but a battle in which goodness and evil were clearly defined.

Have you any idea what communism was? Do you not understand that, vile and horrible as the holocaust was, in numbers of innocent deaths, it pales when compared to the millions of deaths caused by Stalin and Mao Zedong? Do you not understand that communism wasn't some political party you could try and then reject if you didn't like it? Once in, communism was impossible to remove. There was no free speech, no free elections, no freedom of assembly to protest what you saw as bad things and bad people. There was no freedom of religion. Communism, no matter where it was found, was a brutal police state.

In 1948, when Britain could no longer defend Greece from communism, President Harry S. Truman stepped in. With the consent of the non-communist world he pronounced what became known as the Truman Doctrine, which provided aid to nations such as Greece and Turkey, which were threatened by communist takeover. It essentially drew the line in the sand and said to communism, "No farther."

The stakes were freedom or slavery. Make no mistake on that point. Of course there were economic and political considerations, but the central and constant issue was whether we would live freely, or as slaves.

Communism was an attempt at world domination. Let me remind all you "howevers" out there that the Berlin Wall wasn't built to keep the nasty capitalists out but to keep East Germans from leaving. For forty years people in Eastern Europe were held in subjugation. They were jailed, tortured and often killed for speaking their mind. It was this repression that the United States undertook to protect the rest of the world from.

This was a global battle. Every region of the world was involved. It was war, not a boxing match to be played under the Marquess of Queensberry Rules. And it was a war in which only one side's actions came under public scrutiny.

You "howevers" had a field day. I'll tell you why you did. Mortal though the stakes were, those fighting communism always permitted free speech in the fullest.

The United States was damned if it did and damned if it didn't. If it supported odious regimes, such as the Batista dictatorship in Cuba, it was damned for that. Yet the alternative was communism and I remind you that since Castro took over in 1959 there have been thousands of political deaths, thousands of people jailed for their political beliefs and there has never been a free election.

The philosophical battle for the hearts and minds of populations was also a strategic battle. Neither the Soviet Union nor the

United States was prepared to be strategically outflanked. Why was Allende toppled and murdered in Santiago in 1973? Because he was about to take Chile into the communist fold, which would likely have seen some neighbours follow suit. It was tough and dirty but we're talking war here and, as Civil War General William Tecumseh Sherman said, "War is hell."

Did the United States make errors? Of course, it did. Its foreign policy, and that of Britain, in the Iran contra affair of 1987 was stupid and brought about calamities down the road which included Saddam Hussein's move into Kuwait. The refusal of John Foster Dulles to fund the Aswan dam in Egypt in 1956 was a colossal blunder leading to the crisis at the Suez Canal. And there's Vietnam. What a disaster! What's forgotten though is that the United States entered the war in 1964 after the Tonkin Gulf incident to defend the international Geneva agreement that divided the country into North and South Vietnam in 1960.

By 1990 the United States had won the struggle between the two superpowers. But was this a victory of the American bully boys over the Russians? Ask that question of the Poles, the East Germans, the Hungarians, the Romanians, the Czechs and the Slovaks. Ask it of the Bulgarians. Ask the Latvians, the Lithuanians and the Estonians. Ask the citizens of the former Russian republics. Indeed, ask the Russians themselves. Many of these people have had desperately tough times since the Cold War ended but they would never consent to go back to communism.

While you're at it, ask the people of Malaysia and Singapore whether or not they're sorry the British fought the communists there after the war.

What you "howevers" do is an old trick, a verbal conjuring act. First, you take all the sins of the United States out of context and collect them into a one-size-fits-all condemnation. Second, you imply that if the United States had not taken a strong anti-communist stance and stepped in, then the people would have been deliriously happy with what was bound to happen. The Grenadians would have been delighted to live under Castro's

Cuba and Chileans would have loved communism. You want us to believe that Vietnam is a-bursting with democracy thanks to Ho Chi Minh, and that the Sandinistas were freedom-loving democrats. Then, with stunning naiveté you assume that if the United States had simply gone home after the Second World War and let the rest of the world go by, communism would have beat a peaceful retreat.

During the Cold War, the United States and her allies tolerated all you "howevers" marching for peace or for whatever country you thought the United States had last wronged. Meanwhile in the Soviet Union and its satellites no protest was permitted.

When two superpowers tangle, a hell of a lot of other people are going to get bumped and bruised. Great mistakes will be made, such as Russia in Afghanistan and the United States in Vietnam. National dignities will be bruised. Injustices—some very serious—will be committed. But get this all you "howevers" out there—that Sunera Thobani can make an outrageous speech while financed by our government, and the fact that you can echo her sympathies, the fact that I'm here and you can call my program and express your opinion all are due to one thing and one thing only. The United States fought the Cold War and, with precious little help from Canada, won it.

So remember as you shout your anti-American slogans and rewrite history while chanting the latest Noam Chomsky mantra that you owe the right to do so to the country that you so despise and whose martyred dead of September 11 you so basely and so casually dishonour.

HENRY KISSINGER: WAR CRIMINAL OR GENIUS?

Tom Brown (1663–1704), while a student at Christ Church, Oxford, penned these immortal lines:

> I do not love thee, Doctor Fell.
> The reason why I cannot tell;
> But this alone I know full well,
> I do not love thee, Doctor Fell.

So be my thoughts about Dr. Henry Kissinger, for six years the assistant to President Nixon for National Security. During that time Kissinger usurped on a regular basis the powers of the Secretary of State William Rogers, whose job he assumed for three and a half years in 1973. Among his many sins, Dr. Kissinger has been accused of deliberately sabotaging the peace talks with the North Vietnamese in the fall of 1972 in order to help Richard Nixon get re-elected. According to his tormentor, eminent journalist Christopher Hitchens, he cost millions of lives that needn't have been lost. In his best-selling book, *The Trial of Henry Kissinger* (Verso, 2001), Hitchens involves Kissinger in the assassination of Salvatore Allende of Chile, the grief in Bangladesh and East Timor and several other crimes both major and minor.

Dr. Kissinger is a hard man to love and his three volumes of memoirs are notable for what he omits from his interesting, sometimes brilliant, often checkered career. One of the minor aspects of Kissinger's career came back in about 1985 when then Mayor Mike Harcourt tried to prevent him from speaking in Vancouver.

I certainly do not love Dr. Kissinger, but I'm fascinated by him. Many years ago I read his magisterial tome *Diplomacy* (Simon & Schuster, 1994), and have to say that, as a history of diplomacy over the past century and a half, it is brilliant.

For several months I browsed through the good doctor's most recent book, *Does America Need a Foreign Policy? Toward a New Diplomacy for the 21st Century* (Simon and Schuster, 2001) and finally a couple of weeks ago I could no longer resist. It, too, is brilliant as Kissinger roams the world recounting America's position, post Iron Curtain, in each regions. The great man also analyzes in an unusually readable section on a complicated subject, the growth of globalization and the perils it poses. I was surprised at how kindly and understandingly Kissinger views the dissenters and his frank criticism of the United States and the International Monetary Fund.

For an academic whose first language is not English—though he has been in the States since 1938—Henry Kissinger is remarkably easy to read. This makes the complicated world scenes he delves into understandable to people like me who have a limited attention span. Happily, the book has few footnotes to disrupt concentration and, at 288 pages, is not a monumental undertaking.

I don't like Kissinger as a man and there is much about him to find unattractive. He may be, as Hitchens says, a war criminal, as we must always be aware. But he's brilliant, readable and important.

REMEMBRANCE DAY

I remember a lot of things about the Second World War though I was only eight when it began and 14 when it ended. I especially remember Churchill's speech to the Canadian House of Commons on December 30, 1941, where, in response to a warning from the French in June 1940 that in three weeks England's neck would be rung like a chicken, said "some chicken" and then after a suitable pause, "some neck." I remember his speech at the Lord Mayor's Day Luncheon in London on November 10, 1942, where he said, in effect, that Londoners, if offered a respite to the bombing, would say "no ... we will mete out the measure and more than the measure that's been meted out to us."

Most of all, though, I remember Churchill's speech on the Fall of France in July 1940. I'm not sure when I first heard it but probably it was many times during the war. And I've thought of it since so often when I hear the uninspiring, spin-doctored claptrap that comes out of the mouths of so many world leaders these days.

At the Fall of France, with Russia Hitler's ally and the United States choked by isolationism, and with Britain left standing alone against the might of Hitler's armed forces, Churchill went on radio on July 14, 1940, repeating what he had said in the House of Commons:

> Let us therefore brace ourselves to our duties and so bear ourselves that if the British Empire and its Commonwealth last for a thousand years, men will still say: 'This was their finest hour.'

No wonder John Kennedy, upon granting him honorary citizenship in 1964 (the first time since Lafayette) said that Churchill mobilized the English language and marched it off to war.

What I remember most about the war were the big kids, the youngsters who were in Grade 11 and 12 when I was in Grade 6. I especially remember a kid named Clark who came to the first assembly of the year at St. George's School for Boys and took his place alongside his Grade 12 buddies clad in the uniform of the Royal Canadian Air Force. I also remember Bud O'Hara, who despite his Irish name was a cricketer like my dad. I called him Uncle Bud even though he was less than a decade older than me. When he went overseas to fight I wrote to him and he would reply from "somewhere in England," the address the censors required. Uncle Bud went missing over Germany, dead before his twenty-first birthday. I remember the casualty lists that invariably included a friend's older brother or his dad.

I remember these things because these soldiers were all kids. Go to the local senior secondary and take a good look at the kids there. It was kids who acted and looked like these who were killed in the war around the world by the millions. They were kids whose parents couldn't understand them. Their behaviour was, to adult eyes, anti-social if not uncivilized. They had ultra short hair and wore strange clothes with draped trousers. They listened to music their seniors said would take them directly to hell in a handcart.

These kids, or the ones who came back, are the old men and women you see today, in ever decreasing numbers around the cenotaphs and who go from there into veterans' bars for a beer or two to remember.

The question is, do we remember?

We were going to, you know. In the fall of 1945 there were remembrance ceremonies all across Canada. I went to the one at St. Mary's in Kerrisdale to remember my Uncle Howard who was killed in Italy. At these services we all vowed we'd never forget.

You can't expect new generations to understand what their parents, grandparents and great-grandparents accomplished and sacrificed. It happened too long ago for young people to relate. But you can expect that everyone, regardless of age, will make the supreme effort, long after the last veteran has gone, to honour those who made their freedom possible.

The issue at stake during the Second World War was victory or death to all the freedoms we hold dear and death of any who stood in the way of the monsters we were fighting.

Whenever I'm in London I go down to Parliament Square and see the statue of Churchill, leaning on his stick, with jutted jaw looking over to the east whence the Nazi bombers came, defying them to do their worst. I look at St. Paul's Cathedral whose valiant firefighters saved it from certain destruction during the London Blitz. I look all over the city that kept Britain alive long enough for Russia and then the United States to get drawn in, by taking a pasting in 1940 and 1941, and later when the rockets came. I know then why I remember. I remember because I've had a hell of a good life, as have my kids and grandkids thanks to older folks who took it on the chin for me and thanks to young people who were no older than two of my grandchildren are now. You volunteered to die for freedom and you did just that in huge numbers.

And I wonder how we continue to keep this memory alive. Then I pray to God we do, lest by forgetting we doom other generations to make the same sacrifices.

WHO THE HELL WON ANYWAY?

For nearly one half of the twentieth century and for the last third of the nineteenth century, the name of the game for Germany was to gain territory, sometimes to be populated by Germans, sometimes for the safety of a buffer zone, sometimes for "lebensraum." They wanted room to live. Indeed the Second World War was fought precisely to gain territory where Germans could live and prosper. Adolf Hitler could and did blame German re-armament on the Treaty of Versailles, which ended the First World War and which the Germans viewed as a national disgrace. But when Hitler took on the Soviet Union, that excuse went out the window. When Hitler invaded Russia on June 21, 1941, he recaptured all the territories lost by the Treaty of Versailles. He captured much, much more besides. (There is this not terribly noteworthy exception. Germany had lost its colonies in west Africa and islands in the Pacific, which were never seen as that big a deal and scarcely attracted Germans to live there. Germany was so late in the game that her colonies, acquired in the late nineteenth century, were really a financial burden. In the appeasement era of the late 1930s, it was thought that restoration of colonies might satisfy Hitler's appetite. As a negotiating tool it was a non-starter.)

If you look at the bigger picture, the goal of German foreign policy since Bismarck united the country in 1871 was hegemony over central Europe, both in political and economic terms, to create, as Kaiser Wilhelm II phrased it, "a place in the sun."

In 1918, Germany was beaten and humiliated. In 1945 Germany was beaten and humiliated again, though for the first time since the Napoleonic Wars the German population saw war up close. She was devastated and had no chips to play. In the dying days of the Second World War, Germany thought it might gain leverage by throwing its lot in with the western allies against the Soviet Union, but that didn't work. Germany found herself divided into four occupation zones, which eventually became East and West Germany. Germany was without the means by which to support herself. (While the principal industrial area, the Ruhr Valley, remained under the western allies, industry in the Soviet zone was dismantled and taken to Russia by way of reparations. After losing 22 million people one can understand why Russia was in no mood to be generous.)

The Marshall Plan of 1947, named after the American Secretary of State George C. Marshall, provided U.S. aid to European countries and rescued Europe, including Germany, by contributing $12 billion in aid over the next four years. Churchill, in 1946, called for a United States of Europe, starting with a pact between France and West Germany (not ever to include Britain, in Churchill's mind, however) and to the astonishment of all, that happened starting with a coal and steel pact. From this germ of hope came the Common Market, leading to the European Union we see today.

In November 1989, the wall the East German communists built to keep their people from defecting to the west collapsed in every sense of the word and shortly thereafter Germany was re-unified. The Germany that was reunited was not the pre-war Germany of 1939, much less the Germany that preceded the First World War. Many ancient parts of Germany remained under other jurisdictions, mainly in Poland, which, in compensation for land surrendered to Russia, was awarded East Prussia, Pomerania, Silesia and other ancient German territory.

Germany now stands as the strongest country in Europe. France, of course, doesn't admit this but neither does France admit it lost the Second World War and would have lost the First World War (as she lost the Franco-Prussian war of 1870) had it not been for Britain and the United States. Britain knows this to be true, which explains why it has to be dragged kicking and screaming every inch of the way towards a United States of Europe and may never make it.

Germany has been slowed, dramatically, by the costs of taking East Germany back. But that will pass and one day a united Germany will stand as a colossus in the middle of Europe. While under Helmut Kohl Germany accepted the 1945 boundaries, and remembering that all Germans were brutally cast out of what is now Poland, is there any certainty that Germany as the huge power of Europe won't want to re-visit the question of borders?

Once the European Union becomes one political unit, probably with Poland as a member, questions of who owns the ancient territories will be moot. Perhaps.

Starting with Napoleon I, when "bordered" states began to vie for power in a big way, who emerged as the dominant force? The answer is Germany, of course, the power that lost and lost big time in 1945.

But there is one other great question. What will happen next in this great struggle? Will the European Union emerge as a peaceful, "super nation" where ethnicity is a thing of the past? If ethnicity dies as an issue in Europe that nation will certainly be marked as unique in the world, for ethnicity plays such a huge and dangerous role in so many places.

Can we rely on the agreements of this era to govern the next? Maybe. But if we can, it will be the first time in recorded history it's happened. And let's not forget that fifteen years ago a person would have been certified insane for suggesting that the Soviet Union would break up. A little more than twenty-five years ago Gerald Ford probably lost the presidency by claiming Poland wasn't under Russia's thumb.

We hope and are told that the European Union will, by its existence, settle the questions that ravaged Europe over the centuries. I don't believe the borders of Europe have not yet been settled. For the sake of world peace, I fervently hope I'm wrong.

FIVE DAYS IN LONDON

The role of Winston Churchill in the events leading up to the Second World War seem now to be beyond dispute. He warned—and he was ignored—until it was too late. It is widely accepted that Churchill was right to rally his countrymen after he became prime minister of Britain on May 10, 1940, and that in that effort he had his cabinet and Parliament with him. Lately some doubt has been cast by several revisionists who have held that Churchill ought to have made peace with Germany after France was beaten—and that his cabinet wished him to do just that.

Five Days in London (Yale University Press, 2000) by the eminent historian John Lukacs, puts paid to that argument and is thrilling reading to boot. As a reader you are transported to London in those dreadful days when France lay prostrate before the Hun and Britain's army, sans equipment, had barely escaped the Wehrmacht at Dunkirk. Lukacs, a highly regarded American historian, tells the story of May 24–28, 1940. During those five days it was decided whether or not Winston Churchill, who became prime minister on May 10, would remain in power. The plot, for plot the story was, involved three people, Churchill, Neville Chamberlain, whom Churchill had replaced, and Viscount Halifax, whom he had beaten out for the job.

The story of Britain and Churchill in the summer of 1940 has been compromised by wartime propaganda and by those who loved Churchill and those who hated him. The story really starts in the 1930s when Churchill, out of office but a very powerful backbencher in the Conservative caucus, made enemies in his own party on three main issues. He was against home rule for India, he bravely, loyally and stupidly, supported Edward VIII in *l'affaire Wallis Simpson*, and he proved to be horribly right about Adolf Hitler. Churchill made a speech on the debate over the 1938 Munich Agreement that lashed his colleagues, and all who agreed with them, very badly. It made him very unpopular in a country that so dearly wanted to see this agreement as a deliverance from a war they were ill prepared to fight.

Chamberlain and Halifax were appeasers. But Chamberlain finally saw that Hitler was just what Churchill had said he was when Hitler, in March 1939, against the Munich agreement, cynically invaded Prague and the parts of Czechoslovakia he had not got at Munich. Chamberlain, very publicly, had taken Hitler at his word. And by the time war started in September 1939 Chamberlain was good and mad.

At the outset of war, Chamberlain quickly brought Churchill into the cabinet and the inner War Cabinet as First Lord of the Admiralty. By May 1940 the public and the House of Commons were sick of the Conservative government, ironically as it turned out because a botched adventure in Norway for which Churchill bore much responsibility. Churchill, always thirsting for action, and tired of the "phoney war," wanted to stop Germany shipping steel from northern Sweden down the Norwegian coast and ordered the Royal Navy to lay down mines in Norwegian waters. When, on April 9, 1940, Hitler invaded Norway, Churchill saw his chance and largely at his instigation the War Cabinet ordered troops to be landed in two areas. The expeditions were hard to supply and they badly faltered. Though there was enough blame for several ministers, Churchill, as the man in charge of the navy, was much to blame. Very much to his credit, on May 8 when the House debated the famous confidence motion that saw Chamberlain's fall, Churchill wound up the debate with a vigorous defence of his leader, taking his full share of responsibility, and then some, for the Norwegian campaign. Chamberlain took an awful shellacking but won nevertheless with an enormous number of abstainers in the Tory ranks. Because this was at best a hollow victory, Chamberlain knew he could not carry on and that a coalition government of all parties must be formed. But who should lead it? It came down to Churchill and to Halifax, who was handicapped by being in the House of Lords. The answer really came from the Labour Party, which refused to serve under Halifax since Halifax was so clearly one of the pre-war appeasers. Indeed, when Churchill entered the House of Commons on May 13 for the first time as prime minister the applause from the government benches was muted while the Labour benches gave him a warm welcome.

The five days coincided with the very worst moments of the war for Britain. The British Expeditionary Force had been cut off and surrounded on three sides, with their back to the sea at Dunkirk. Churchill reckoned that it would be a miracle if 50,000 men were saved. In the event it was a miracle—335,000 were saved though virtually all equipment was lost.

During that five days, Halifax wanted to continually explore peace opportunities. Churchill saw that peace would only come on Hitler's terms. Chamberlain, dying of cancer, was the only other Tory in the five-man War Cabinet, the Labourites being Arthur Greenwood and Clement Attlee, so he was the deciding factor. Chamberlain, courageously and without concern that he had been ousted in favour of Churchill, took Churchill's side. Is it too much to say, then, that the much-pilloried Chamberlain, by his selflessness and foresight, saved Britain and the world?

From May through to the end of September 1940 Churchill encouraged the "peace party," Halifax, R. A. B. Butler and others, to keep handing out peace feelers especially through contacts in neutral Sweden. He let it be known to the peace seekers that he would make a deal with Hitler. But he never intended to. He was simply buying time knowing that if Hitler didn't invade Britain before the end of October he would have to wait another eight months and, who knows, perhaps the Americans would by then be involved.

This wasn't just Churchill bravery and pugnacity—though he possessed no small measure of those qualities—but his ability to see the bigger picture. If Britain made a deal with Hitler, Russia would be his next movement. Coming off Russia's difficult time putting down the Finns the previous winter, Churchill perceived that Hitler could beat Russia, bringing under German's control the oil fields of Persia, where the Royal Navy got its oil, and the gateway to India. Churchill, who very early had taken the measure of the man, knew that Hitler wouldn't hesitate to attack Britain once Russia was disposed of. And apart from all else, what would this do to the policy of the United States? They would be forced to concentrate their interest on the Far East, not a Britain that had laid down and died.

By every measure, Churchill was right and his decision to stand alone, and the British resolve to support him, saved, by a thread, western civilization—thanks to the "Man of Munich," Neville Chamberlain.

PAST, PRESENT
AND FUTURE

LAWYERS AND JUDGES:
SACRED COWS NO MORE?

I practised law starting in 1961, retiring to go into politics in 1975. I was always very proud of my profession—it was an honourable profession. I also had a profound respect, which is not to say awe, for the court system.

I use the past tense because a quarter century of looking at the legal "game" from another perch gives quite a different perspective, especially to one who used to play the game. Law is now big business and a badly run, hyper greedy business at that, whereas not so very long ago it was a profession with a business side.

Let me explain. Everything we do has in mind the fact that we would like to earn a living. And very few of us are prepared to take a Franciscan vow of poverty. But when I practised, lawyers had not yet become hostage to the International Business Machine Corporation, better known as IBM. The slavery of the profession to a computer master had just begun when I left. With the computer came the ability to instantly record every minute spent on a client's business—with that ability came the reality. Indeed, with the computer came the lawyer's penchant for cheating his client.

How strange it is when I think on it. In 1974 my Kamloops firm had just installed a telex machine so we could, by typing a few words, send information to others on the telex system. A guy with a ridiculous crewcut used to advertise for telex on television for CN-CP and it was so very modern. How could communication get any more modern than that? Now even the fax, which replaced the telex, is passé. Everything is online, hugely efficient and even more hugely expensive.

It was only a few years ago that lawyers could still take cases they wanted to take and the hell with the money. Of course they couldn't take too many of them—the banker, always your partner, insisted that you meet your loan requirements. But, dammit, you did a fair amount of work just because you really believed that it was important that it be done.

There's an inexorable drive by every lawyer to keep the billings high in the internal competition that determines who will be a partner, and which law firm will survive and which will die. The computer has all but driven the humanity from the practice of law. The duty to serve the client—indeed the very taking on of a client—has become a matter of money and no more.

The lawyer has gone from being a person who society respects to one who is—and I don't think I exaggerate—if not despised, then held in very low esteem.

The interesting thing is that lawyers don't understand this, not yet. A once honourable profession looks more and more like the oldest profession on earth.

How sad it is, for never has there been such a need for "mouthpieces" who are skilled in putting to those in authority the case of those ground down by the system and the huge bureaucracy it has spawned. And as this need ever grows, the services required are pushed out of reach of everyone but the corporate client who has money and tax write-offs to burn.

I'm glad I was around to see the practice of law as it was when duty to client and justice still meant something to those with the monopoly of access to the judge.

The bench has fared little better. The high esteem in which judges were traditionally held has fallen, if not tumbled. Judges are feeling this change in status and in consequence are complaining a lot lately. In fact, they've become a bunch of whiners. A murmur of dissent from a politician or the media and one of their ilk leaps onto the front page of the newspaper chanting mantras about the sanctity of the judge's prerogatives to judge without fear or favour. When the judge is through, the lawyers chime in with their vigorous defence. Indeed what else would you expect from the lawyers who need the goodwill of the judges on a day-to-day basis?

"But the poor dears can't defend themselves," seems to be the rationale. Really? Judges seem to be defending themselves just fine. What they don't offer is decent explanations for their behaviour, nor for the entire damned justice system they administer.

I have had personal experience that would leave a saint a bit cynical about the justice system. But that experience is outweighed by more than twenty years of hearing the public comment on the justice system. I now question what I was brainwashed into believing as a law student, then as a practising lawyer for fifteen years—that the judge is beyond reproach. I was told the judge is not to be criticized other than over a quiet beer with other lawyers. If you think the judge screwed up, then appeal. And if your client can't afford to appeal, then the lawyer's phrase came into play, "Impecuniosity is no excuse."

If the judge has misbehaved, as opposed to simply making a lousy judgment, why all you need do is convince the Judicial Council who have the right to take the matter to the Parliament of Canada and have him removed from office. Right. The fact that this has never happened and never will should not, of course, deter you.

What lawyers, be they practitioners or judges, refuse to acknowledge is that the whole bloody business is so expensive that even the well-to-do cannot challenge even egregiously erroneous findings. The law is now for the large corporations or the very rich, or damned fools. A famous cartoon, by J. Bright, first published in an eighteenth-century magazine and now seen in many lawyers' offices (in a room clients don't frequent) shows a cow labelled "Litigation." Pulling on the tether is the plaintiff and pulling on the tail is the defendant. Meanwhile milking the cow is the lawyer. Two centuries ago Voltaire refused his lawyer's advice to sue by saying, "I was never ruined but twice: once when I lost a lawsuit, and once when I won one." Imagine what he would say today!

How well I remember studying the law of damages. The law in its majesty says that it is the duty of the injured party to mitigate his or her damages. Shorn of the legalese it means that if your ship is sunk or your truck destroyed by the fault of another, thus you can't deliver your cargo, you must forthwith get another boat or truck and fulfill your contract. You can't complain that you can't afford to buy or rent another boat or truck because again, as the lawyers so succinctly put it, "Impecuniosity is no excuse." So neat and tidy, that. It's not up to the judges or lawyers to recognize the real world. If someone else hurts you, and perhaps even because of that act you can't "mitigate" your loss, too bad for you.

This is what the law will not recognize—life in the real world. Courts run up the expense without any regard whatever for the cost. In my own case, the hearing on increased maintenance was started and stopped at least five times. The adjournments were never to suit my convenience; I wanted the matter concluded. No, siree, it was the judges and lawyers whose convenience was to be met, at enormous cost to my pocketbook.

The notion that, if dissatisfied, you can "tax" your lawyer's bill is another illusion. To do this you must hire another lawyer who, of course, will first, at $300 per hour, review your case. Then you must pay him or her, probably a minimum of $1,000, usually much more, to appear before a registrar to fight the case. This is one great big brother and sisterhood we're dealing with here, folks.

A partial answer to the complaint about cost is an expansion of the small claims procedure. If the matter in issue is $10,000 or less you can get a hearing before a small claims court without a lot of fuss, and where the arcane rules of evidence are relaxed. There most matters are settled at a mandatory settlement conference. Not only is a lawyer not needed, it is contraindicated because no court costs are involved. Moreover, the lower order of judges tends to dislike lawyers cluttering their proceedings. They are naturally more down to earth and closer to real people than their red-robed brethren who dine at the best of clubs with their old lawyer pals.

Why shouldn't the small claims limit be increased to $100,000 or more, for that matter? And why shouldn't all marital matters be handled in family court, without lawyers, leaving it to the judge to appoint a lawyer to help if the case gets too heavy? Why not, as former Chief Justice Bryan Williams of the B.C. Supreme Court has suggested, expand the role of mediation and arbitration? In short, why not do everything humanly possible to get lawyers the hell out of a case?

Other countries, notably Japan and many European countries, get along with fewer lawyers than we in British Columbia alone are stuck with.

But, you might ask, weren't you a lawyer yourself once? I bet you charged what the traffic would bear. Guilty on both counts. But it takes one to know one. It takes a lawyer who once charged 20 percent (it's now up to 40 percent) of a damages award to know the system well enough to criticize it. And that was for doing what a client could easily, in most cases, have done independently had the procedures not been so damned complicated.

The old adage applies: "Justice delayed is justice denied." What the judicial system refuses to recognize is that delaying justice is what pads the wallets of those in it. Every adjournment is money in the bank to the lawyers doing the adjourning. When a third party pays the bills, the case never ends until that party's funds or patience is exhausted. There's the old story of a judge in a wills case looking down on the squabbling lawyers, always knowing that their costs would be paid out of the estate, saying, "It would be a shame to waste this estate on the beneficiaries."

To find the fat in your legal bill, look at the disbursements. Every phone call is automatically billed out at one-tenth of an hour. (For a $300 per hour lawyer that's $30 a pop.) How often does a phone call last six minutes? In fact, most calls are billed at

0.3 to cover the secretary getting your file for the lawyer so your lawyer's thirty-second call to another lawyer on a routine matter costs you ninety bucks. It's a huge scam!

The judges who complain about being complained about, are, unwittingly perhaps, stern gatekeepers at what should be a storehouse of public knowledge. We don't understand the legal system because those in it don't want us to. Judges could order that adjournments be at the lawyer's expense. They could pay attention to the pleadings and the hugely lengthy examinations for discovery and other pre-trial evidence taken and penalize lawyers for prolixity and verbosity. They won't, of course, because they were once in the game themselves and they must meet their brethren at the club, at a bar dinner or at a common watering hole.

It's not an active conspiracy; it's so age old that those in it don't ever think about it. To them it's as natural as one medical doctor never testifying against another. It's bred in them from the day they enter law school that they are in a sacred brotherhood with its own incantations, costumes and time-sanctified rituals, whose high priests must not only always be protected but who in turn have their own duty to protect their protectors.

As H. L. Mencken once said, "Injustice is relatively easy to bear; what stings is justice."

It's a bloody scandal whose denouement is long past due.

Respecting Mental Health

No one would mock someone in a wheelchair or on crutches or allude to a disfiguring scar or birthmark. Yet personal insult seems to be quite in order when mental health is at issue.

Politicians and columnists alike remark, "They must have forgotten to take their medication," to make the point that someone they don't like at the moment must have taken leave of his senses. These are often well-known people who would never dream that they're being offensive trying to be droll. Margaret Wente of the *Globe and Mail* and Sondra Gotleib in the *National Post* wrote articles in 2002 that referred to drugs such as Prozac and Paxil as if they were some kind of jolly tranquilizers. Droll they thought they were—droll they were not. They have no idea how offensive they really were.

Even worse, best-selling authors such as John Shelby Spong in his fascinating book, *A New Christianity for a New World: Why Traditional Faith Is Dying and How a New Faith Is Being Born* (HarperCollins, 2001), discuss depression as something to be treated by drugs, including alcohol. They show no appreciation at all for the fact that much depression has a physical cause, a shortage of serotonin, which medicines (not "drugs") replace.

Not long ago it was reported in one of Canada's national newspapers that we've seen a 35 percent increase in mental illness in recent years and that, reported and treated or not, somewhere between one fifth and one quarter of all Canadians suffer from depression or will before they die.

We who suffer this ailment also know that the biggest barrier to getting treatment is the social stigma still attached to mental illness. This stigma even has an official aspect to it. Why are there "mental" health statutes, "mental" health organizations and "mental" health institutions? Why is there this division between "mental" health and "physical" health?

But the main battle is against the subtle stigma. Schizophrenia, a hugely disabling and distressing illness has nothing to do with "split" personalities, yet the word is wrongly used to mean just that. (In a strange way, people who use the word in this way are actually correct. It's sort of like that marvellous movie of a decade ago, *Victor/Victoria* (1982), in which a male impersonated a woman who in turn impersonated a man. It is not inaccurate to use the word "schizophrenic" to indicate a "split" personality. It's just that in medical terms schizophrenia has come to mean something quite different.)

Prozac has been a marvellous medicine for many people, yet the word is used as an epithet. "Why don't you take your Prozac?" the ignorant say, to suggest that some behaviour by the object of their disaffection would be changed for the better by taking what they see to be a mind-altering drug, when really Prozac is a medicine. It is thoughtless to imply, however much in jest, that it is otherwise. Some professions, the law, politics and journalism, for example, desire to hurt with words. Surely, though, it should not be the object to wound innocent bystanders.

Depression is not only widely prevalent among Canadians, it is also, more often than not, eminently treatable. The problem is getting sufferers to see a doctor and onto proper medications. The stigma, I can assure you from personal experience, is very real. Men especially find it hard to admit that they are depressed; it doesn't accord with the image they think society has of them.

People who joke about this usually mean no harm but they do harm nevertheless, great harm, especially if they are public figures. As long as the image of the mental patient is that implied by trite and ill thought-out remarks, depressed people will not seek help. And that's a tragedy.

What compounds this tragedy is that even when a person decides to seek help it just might not be available. If a person with a serious stomach ache or a broken limb were treated by the health care system in the same way a mental health victim is treated, then there would be blood in the streets and the legislature would be stormed. Emergency wards are not equipped to help mental health victims and, even worse, neither is the medical profession. People with deep depression will wait forever for someone to see them at hospital; when they reach their doctor they will rely on the doctor's good nature, for doctors are not afforded enough time under the Medical Services Plan to properly diagnose and treat mental health patients. You can't blame the doctor who tells a patient to go home, hum a few bars of "Land of Hope and Glory" and drink a stiff Scotch—there is simply not enough incentive for the family physician to take the extra courses on depression to get up to speed and stay there. I'm happy to say that many doctors do make the sacrifice but I can tell you, at the risk of embarrassing her, the story of Dr. Theresa Hogarth.

Dr. Hogarth was, for many years, a general practitioner practising in New Westminster, British Columbia. She became interested in mental health, especially depression, to the point that the majority of her patients were in this field. Put bluntly, she found that even though she was run off her feet, she couldn't make a living. Tragically for all her patients and those she took the time to help on my radio show, Theresa took a high-paying job in the drug industry in Toronto.

This means a number of things. If the patient is not like I was, lucky enough to have a family doctor who knew and understood depression, he will get bad advice at best. In all likelihood he will be referred to a psychiatrist and that will take a minimum of six months. Imagine! A man—for males are most prone to suffer the stigma—has finally, after agonizing suffering, summoned up the courage to see a doctor and he's told that diagnosis and treatment will be at least six months off. Not to put too fine a point on it, the entry into the health care system for the mentally ill is often medieval. The great tragedy, of course, comes with the young and the far too many teenage suicides that blot our escutcheon.

The government of British Columbia has, to its credit, appointed a Minister of State for Mental Health. (Unfortunately, his first act was to abolish the position of the Mental Health Advocate who was able to do what the government was unable to do, and patients unwilling to do, namely identify where the problems were.) It would seem that the government is talking the talk but is unwilling to walk the walk.

The problem remains an elementary one, though no easier of solution. A stigma remains attached to mental illness, the gate to help is hard to open and sometimes shut tight, and when the gate is pried open, diagnosis and treatment too often are mixed and uncertain.

Pressure must be brought to bear on the government so that doctors can spend the appropriate time with patients and be paid appropriately. This means that general practitioners must educate themselves in this important field of medicine. And the public, especially those in the media, must work and work hard at nullifying the stigma. For this to happen, employers and trade unions must make it easier for employees to enter the system by recognizing that there is no more shame in being a depression patient than being a diabetic (I happen to be both). Many companies and unions are now recognizing that, quite apart from the humanitarian considerations—and they must always be important—every employee is an investment of time, effort and money. I'm convinced that much alcoholism is people with depression self-medicating. Employers must learn the signs of depression and be prepared to show the way to help. For of all the tragedies I have mentioned, perhaps the greatest is that many depressed people never find out that after proper diagnosis and treatment, the results can often be little short of miraculous.

Please don't misunderstand what I'm about to say in conclusion as immodest. I want to emphasize my point by saying that since I was diagnosed and began treatment fifteen years ago I have hosted a daily radio show, prepared an editorial for each program plus two more per week for my website, done as many as three newspaper columns a week, written scores of other articles, given dozens of speeches and written four books. The person saved from the ravages of depression is worth the effort.

The Cost of Medical Gizmos

It was a troubling article I read, about a year ago, in the London *Sunday Times*, that told of a miraculous cure for Parkinson's disease. Well, not exactly a cure but a technique that banishes all the manifestations of the dread ailment. It's an electronic implant in the brain that removes the shaking and restores muscular control. It is, in fact, a miracle for those who suffer the disease. But there's a snag. Each treatment costs $50,000. In Canada approximately 100,000 people have the disease. You do the math on the cost to government for medical care with the electronic implant. It's awesome.

But the electronic gizmo for Parkinson's disease is merely the harbinger of things to come. We will surely soon see mechanical organs to complement organ transplants, the expense of which will be horrendous.

One of the problems with our medicare system is that we've never come to grips with defining what we, as a society, are prepared to pay for out of the public purse. Are there any limits? If there are, what are they and who decides them?

These questions have immediate implications because modern techniques are not only scarce, they're expensive as hell. Doctors have, until now, decided who qualifies for organ transplants based on what they believe to be medically sound factors. If you were not in otherwise good health you wouldn't get a new heart or lungs, for example. Because until recent times organ transplants were so rare, no one thought to question medical decisions. Now, however, we have surgeons in Australia refusing heart and lung transplants to smokers on the ground that these organs are rarely available for transplant and ought to go only to those who don't abuse their bodies. Civil libertarians take issue and ask how doctors can make moral as well as medical judgments. It surely can't be long before the Charter of Rights and Freedoms is invoked on behalf of an elderly smoker who seeks a heart transplant.

But it's not just in the area of spectacular surgery that decisions will have to be made. Everything is getting so expensive. How do we ration diagnostic services as more and more of us want magnetic resonance imaging (MRIs) as a matter of course and of right? How do we determine who will and will not be referred to a specialist as people see that referral as a right, not something to be left up to the general practitioner? And, what if we don't like that specialist's opinion, or don't have confidence in it? Can we ask for yet another tax paid referral?

It would seem that there is very little we can't cure. Will our poor old publicly financed health system be required to fund every spectacular cure that biomedical research spawns? The benefits need to be credited against the costs. For example, if Christopher Reeves and all who suffer paralysis could be returned to normal lives, the savings not only in medical but in social terms would be enormous.

Medicare will come under financial attack because of the success of medical science and the expectations both new techniques and free medicine raise. Until now, very few new techniques have not been publicly financed. We have become used to seeing new medical miracles available "for free." The trick is to decide what to fund before it's too late for rational debate.

Perhaps it is too late already. Rationing of services has been tackled in Oregon, for example, where it is done by a public process. But Canadians expect all medical procedures, however spectacular and expensive, to be fully funded and woe to the political party who would suggest otherwise.

I fear that we will be forced to accept private sector involvement in what used to be a publicly funded system, with the private sector, not the Canadian public, calling the shots.

THE GENOME PROJECT: DO WE REALLY WANT TO KNOW?

The genome project, carried out by scientists all over the world and very much at the University of British Columbia has mapped our genes and can tell us more about ourselves than, I argue here, we may really want to know. From this genome map all will be clear even, perhaps, when we will die and what we will die of.

I wonder if the significance of the genome project is fully appreciated? I know that it's boggled my mind, but then I have the least scientific mind in the universe. The thought that all my ailments past, present and especially future can be mapped is too big an idea to get my mind around even though I've had the opportunity of interviewing the late Dr. Michael Smith, UBC's Nobel laureate, several times on the subject. He, I might say, had many doubts about many of the moral questions raised and it's so sad we lost him before he recorded these concerns as he told me he would someday do.

I am amazed at being able to know just what your medical predispositions are. Dr. Smith gave the example of the late Jack Webster, who smoked three packs of cigarettes a day for nearly a lifetime yet lived to eighty-one while others get lung cancer far earlier with much less smoking. Will gene mapping solve that paradox? The answer is almost certainly yes. But of course gene mapping is much more than that. At age thirty-five, say, you could know what sort of diseases you will be prone to and even what you will likely die of and when. What may be even more chilling is that your employer, the government and your insurance company are able to know these things, too. George

Orwell's "Big Brother" has arrived, but he is not only in the government, not by a long shot.

Let's take insurance for example—you buy both disability and life insurance to offset the disasters that come with early illness or death. This insurance is sold based upon probabilities. At thirty-five, say, your premium will be based upon a number of factors, including lifestyle and when and how your parents and siblings died, if they are deceased, what diseases run in your family, your general physical health and so on. From this package of information the insurance company makes its underwriting decisions and either insures you or it doesn't. If it insures you, it sets the appropriate premium. The vast majority of us carry our disability and life insurance through group plans where we work and the ability of the insurer to decline is lessened by the fact that the group is so large that many of our personal peculiarities are often overlooked or not even requested.

But what happens when insurance companies have the ability to know, damned near for certain, how long we're going to live and with much greater certainty than now, when we might have a disabling stroke or heart attack? Will that mean, for example, that normal life insurance will no longer be available and that accidental death or injury is all you'll be able to insure against?

Isn't this going to mean that many people who are now insurable because their apparent weaknesses are poorly predictable, would become uninsurable because of a gene map prediction? What company, given a gene map showing that largely because of heredity you are in grave danger of a stroke at fifty, is going to give you disability insurance until you retire? Would insurance companies then only insure the better risks—admittedly at much lower cost to the insured person? Who then picks up the tab for the uninsured people who are suddenly unemployable and, but for the gene chart, would be collecting disability insurance?

This, of course, raises the bigger question of privacy. Under what circumstances must you disclose your gene chart? Must you

135

submit, as a condition of employment or as a condition of insurance or perhaps a pilot's licence or even a driver's licence, to such a test?

And who owns the results of this test? Suppose you want this done on a physician's advice, can this be subpoenaed as evidence in a trial, for example? Does it go with the rest of your medical records, which for good reason you already might feel compelled to protect?

Do you want to know at age thirty-five that, for reasons beyond your control, you're likely a goner at age fifty? Some would say yes, I suppose, so that they could plan for their families. Many more of us, I suspect, would rather stay in our somewhat troubled but understandable state of denial.

This modern age of immense medical change has left us with many social and ethical issues with which to grapple. Unhappily, for Canadians at least, they come at a time when government is especially remote from their control and the bureaucracy's natural appetite for whatever information it can collect on individuals seems insatiable.

QUESTIONS OF SCIENCE

Genetically modified foods and caged fish farms have something in common: the onus of proof is on the wrong party. The onus is on the public to prove that genetically modified foods and caged fish are harmful. Instead the onus should be on the companies, and on science itself to prove beyond a reasonable doubt—in the case of genetically modified foods I would argue beyond a shadow of a doubt—that what they propose will do no harm. To make matters worse, the judge is on the take.

I cut my environmental teeth on Rachel Carson's classic, *Silent Spring* (Houghton Mifflin, 1962), which has recently been reprinted in hard cover. Carson exposed, to the surprise of the public and the horror of the scientific world that, among other things, DDT was running amok in the environment. DDT was one of the wonder chemicals of the Second World War along with sulpha drugs and penicillin. These latter discoveries had so advanced the ability to cure infection that there was the feeling that medical science could do no wrong. I well remember the early days of television watching documentaries on DDT that showed scientists in white lab coats telling us that soon the world would be free of pests thanks to this wonder compound. It didn't seem to occur to these scientists to ask whether or not these pests had a role to play in nature's scheme of things or to concern themselves with any problems DDT might incidentally cause. As we now know, one of those problems was to so weaken eggshells that we damn near lost the bald eagle population of the West Coast.

Men in white lab coats also told us that thalidomide was a dandy remedy for morning sickness, that IUD devices were great contraceptive devices, that tobacco was, if not good for you, at least harmless and that aspartame is the perfect substitute for sugar.

The money to be made, if the truth of these and other scientific assertions are accepted, is mind-boggling. Tobacco, for God's sake, now condemned by all science, is making more sales worldwide than ever before. Where there's money, there's political influence. The Canadian Pharmaceutical Association, headed by a former Liberal cabinet minister, Judy Erola, is probably the most effective lobby group in the country. They are joined by Cargill, Westons and other agricultural mega-corporations in promoting the hell out of aspartame, genetically modified foods and ocean-based fish farms so that governments, who receive political donations from them, are like judges on the take. The consumer hasn't got a chance unless we stand our ground and fight like hell.

When that does happen, we face contempt and ridicule and find that we must somehow, virtually without funds, prove that these scientific miscreants in the white lab coats are wrong.

If we the public don't start practising not only a lot of skepticism but applying a lot of political pressure as well, we may be facing a worldwide crisis that will make global warming pale in insignificance. For if science is wrong about genetically modified foods, and genetically modified grain is planted all over the world, then the resulting catastrophe will be irreversible.

The Emperor Has No Clothes

Not long ago I got to discussing modern art with a guest on my radio show, the managing director of the Barbican Art Centre in London. I immediately went to the jugular and asked him about the New Tate Gallery, which is across the Thames from the Barbican and, I must say, not associated with it. In the New Tate, which incidentally draws huge crowds, exceeding the main Tate on Milbank, there are some extraordinary exhibits under the name "art." One is a toilet bowl. Then in December 2001 I read about Israel Mora, the Mexican performance artist who obtained public funds, both Mexican and Canadian, for masturbating into vials. How in hell can that be art? Well, it seems that it depends upon who puts the toilet bowl there, and one assumes, who's whacking himself off. If it is a person of talent, then he is speaking to us through this art and it therefore becomes, if not a masterpiece, at least a very valuable addition to the gallery. Indeed we are lucky to have such treasures in our midst.

This brings to mind the American artist Barnett Newman's famous painting *Voice of Fire*, which the National Gallery of Canada purchased on March 7, 1990, for $1.8 million, considered a great bargain. The painting consisted of three large stripes painted diagonally on a large piece of plywood. In outrage, a farmer in Manitoba painted three diagonal stripes on a piece of plywood three-quarters the size of *Voice of Fire* and offered it to the National Gallery for three-quarters of a million dollars. For reasons that escape me, this generous offer was declined.

The artsy fartsy crowd that defend art of this kind say they are appointed by the government to make independent choices and thus should not be interfered with. The corollary is, of course, that interference by the paymaster, the state, amounts to censorship. None of us much likes censors, bureaucratic pointy-heads that they are. But aren't we talking about the public purse here and how it should be spent? Don't we, as a group of taxpayers, have the right to say "Stuff and nonsense! This is crap. The emperor has no clothes. We are being duped into believing that utter nonsense such as toilet bowls, cum juice and coloured stripes are things of great, and expensive, artistic merit. If the private sector wants to spend its ill-gotten gains on such foolishness, fine and dandy, but leave me, the taxpayer, out of it."

This becomes a thorny question because it brings into focus state subsidies of the arts. If the state can arbitrarily reject art because the public thinks it's foolish, then where does it end? Following that argument, the early and traditional art of Picasso would be appropriate for state purchase but none of his modern work would be. That work, incidentally, passed Picasso's own definition that "art is what sells." (Interesting defence of the marketplace by a communist, I always thought!)

It's a tough question. Does the state subsidize a symphony orchestra but not a rock band? If so, why the distinction? The fact is that the state does distinguish when it comes to outright subsidies but it subsidizes all noise called music through its Canadian content rules.

I will stray from my usual intense dislike of anything that smacks of government censorship to say that stripes on plywood, vials of semen and stray toilet bowls are not art suitable for public subsidy. What governments across the land ought to do is appoint someone to defend common sense, a person to be called the "Senseperson." This Senseperson would be selected by the House of Commons or legislature, as the case may be, as is the ombudsman in British Columbia, and must have unanimous approval of the legislative committee set up to vet the applications. Thereafter the Senseperson would report not to government but to the legislature as a whole.

This job should have wide powers to look at all government expenditures and declare whether they are sense or nonsense.

Such a person would earn his salary in the first five minutes in office. Hell, he'd only have to look at a picture or two and he could save years of his cost right off the bat.

This, surely, is an idea whose time has come!

Growing Up in a "Rural City"

I don't know what it was that got me thinking. Maybe it was going down to Granville Island and remembering how that used to be an industrial stinkhole when I was a kid. Maybe that made me think of the old Lonsdale Quay, which when I was a boy was a shipyard, building ships of war. I used to take the North Van ferry there with my pals for a Saturday trek up Lynn Creek, where we did as routine all the things that are now, for sensible safety reasons, expressly forbidden. I began to realize that I've been around for a very long time and can remember a very different city.

I grew up in Kerrisdale before it was tony. At the top of McCleery Street where I lived was a working dairy farm owned by Baroness Van Steenwyck, a Dutch lady who, to the great fun of all the kids in the neighbourhood, was visited in about 1944 by Holland's then Princess, later Queen, Juliana. We all somehow wound up with little Dutch flags, I'm damned if I know where from.

Behind our house was a woods almost two square blocks in size. It was a superb place for forts, hiding and playing doctor with little girls.

My friend Denis and I used to go down to the Musqueam Reserve and fish in Tin Can Creek and Pee Wee Creek, where we caught small cutthroat trout. One day in the fall an Indian kid, maybe sixteen years old, came by with a gaff, hooked two big coho from under the bank, and gave me one. I couldn't believe that such fish could exist in so tiny a stream. Thus I learned an important lesson about coho and where they spawn. When I got the fish home and showed it to my father he thought that I was lying and had stolen it.

On nice days, Denis and I would go to Wreck Beach for a swim. We were, I suppose, among the first of the nude swimmers that the beach became famous for in later years.

We had rural sounds, then, too. I would lie awake in the morning and hear birds, hundreds of them: robins, Stellars' jays and chickadees and the steady staccato of the woodpecker. In the fall, I would hear the guns of the bird shooters off Lulu Island and the fog horn at Point Atkinson.

We had bad things, too, like a war that so frequently brought bad news to our friends and our family with Uncle Howard, killed in Italy. And we had polio, then called infantile paralysis, which was an annual scare of huge and well-remembered proportions.

I remember some red letter days, too, such as when my dad came to our summer place at Granthams Landing and told us that Pier "D" had burned down in a huge conflagration that brought most of the citizenry downtown to see it. That was 1936. I remember King George V's Silver Anniversary and the big parade in 1935 and the even bigger one the next year for Vancouver's fiftieth birthday with Mayor Telford riding in the big open convertible and candy tossed to the kids. I remember when King George VI and Queen Elizabeth, the late Queen Mom, came to town in May 1939 to make sure we were all "at Britain's side whate'er betide" as things got a bit sticky in Europe.

The big deal for us as kids was to go down Marine Drive to Hyland Barnes Nursery and pluck weeds for a dime an hour. Or we took the Interurban to Lulu Island and weeded at Eddie's Nurseries for the same lofty wages. We were lucky to last two hours but in the 1930s a movie cost a dime, as did a double-decker cone, or a milk shake, or a soda. When the war came and an entertainment tax drove the price of a Saturday movie to twelve cents, we all had to get a raise in allowance.

Funny what you remember about money. The wonderful thing about meeting a godfather or a favourite uncle was that when he shook your hand his hand had a quarter, or perhaps even a fifty-cent piece in it! That was a hell of a lot of money when $75 a month was a living wage. We all saved shinplasters (twenty-five-cent banknotes).

Saturday, except in the summer, was the big day. If you were a little kid—under ten years old—you walked up to the Kerrisdale Theatre on 41st Avenue for the matinee. It often featured a serial such as *King of the Royal Mounted*, who, as I recall, always had some damned faithful dog whose name I've forgotten at his side. There was always a contest, too—for a yo-yo or a bolo bat—and I never get close to winning. Hell, I couldn't even sell enough *Liberty* magazines to get the neat compass offered, much less earn the great two-wheel bike with the V-shaped handlebars and balloon tires.

We had streetcars, then, and it was better. Mail came twice a day and once on Saturday. We had a milkman and a bread man who came by horse-drawn wagon—I kid you not—so that horse buns and their odour were part of life in the suburbs. Other home deliveries included the egg man and a "Chinaman" who delivered fruit and vegetables in an old Model "T" Ford truck. We didn't think of "Chinaman" as a pejorative term; we used it because the white community accepted them, quite wrongly of course, as inferiors. "Japs" fished and "Hindus" (actually Sikhs) delivered wood and "Chinamen" delivered groceries. Times were uncomplicated by concern for political correctness. Our "Chinaman" was Low Yow, a delightful man of indeterminate age who used to send me grapes and dates, as a gift, when I had the measles or mumps or whatever childhood disease was going around. Many home deliveries were made by horse drawn sled in the winter, for in those days Vancouver had several weeks of snow. It was great fun for kids, who would sleigh down Macdonald hill to the "flats," where all the dairy farms were, or on Quilchena Golf Club (the old one at 33rd and Pine Crescent), or on Tolmie Hill.

Those were the days of great loyalties. There were no shopping centres. You went to butchers such as James Inglis Reid on Granville near Pender with his slogan, "We ha'e meat that ye can eat." If you were a Jersey Farm person you didn't buy from Turner's Dairy. You were either a Shelley's 4X bread person or you bought from McGavin's. The same loyalties were given to the companies that delivered sawdust for the furnace and ice, if you didn't have a fridge (though our family as long as I could remember had a Kelvinator refrigerator).

Most of us burned sawdust delivered by Morrow Ice and Coal but sometime toward the end of the war we switched to coal with an Iron Fireman furnace. The logo showed an "iron fireman" filling the coal hamper. After the furnace arrived at our house it transpired that I would play the fireman, loading the hamper and then taking the "clinkers" out with a claw-like weapon.

Morrow, who delivered the coal, too, had a marvellous slogan: "Phone to Morrow for your coal today."

And, yes, we had a phone. The number was Kerrisdale 2780. If your number had a letter attached that was a social downer for it meant you had a party line, sharing with three or four neighbours. The phone number for one set of my cousins, whose dad was overseas putting the family in straitened conditions, was Kerrisdale 2389R. He knew and felt the slight. There were no dials, Touch-Tone or otherwise. "Central" answered when you picked up the phone and said, "Number, pu-leeese." I liked it better than whatever ghastly form of recorded human voice now comes over your phone at you.

We had radios in those days and as kids we got to listen to the daytime soaps when we stayed home sick. Even if it was a year between provident illnesses—being sick with one of the childhood diseases was considered fun you looked forward to—you could tune in to the soap opera and it was as if nothing had happened in the interval. I remember very well *The English Family Robinson*, which was a British soap about a wartime English family whose son was "one of the few" in the Battle of Britain. There was *Oxydol's Own Ma Perkins* (a real soap). Rinso's ("Rinso

White! Rinso White! Happy Little Washday Song!") *Big Sister*. And Ivory Soap (99 and 44/100s percent pure) had a "soap" opera, *The O'Neills*, while Lifebuoy did *Gangbusters*, which wasn't a soap but a kids' afternoon and evening program. And, of course, there was *Lux Presents—Hollywood* with Cecil B. De Mille. There were the afternoon classics of Jack Armstrong, the "All American Boy." These shows tended towards cereals—Jack's poison was Wheaties, not available in Canada to our annoyance—we who so badly wanted the great adventures its consumption implied. *Terry and the Pirates* was brought to you by "Quaker Puff Wheat Sparkies, the Wheat That's Shot from Guns! Here Comes Quaker with a Bang Bang! Rat-a-tat tat Bang Bang!" There was Captain Marvel, who in real life was Billy Batson, the newspaper kid. He made the metamorphosis by shouting "Shazam!" And, of course the mild-mannered Clark Kent, who became Superman. There was *Little Orphan Annie* and her blank eyes with the equally blank-eyed Daddy Warbucks, Punjab, The Asp, and, of course, the faithful dog Sandy. During the war we all joined Annie's Junior G-Men and got her "How to Fly" kit.

We also were members of other important clubs. We were Shelley's 4X kids in my neighbourhood and that put us in touch with a famous cowboy—I've forgotten which now, maybe it was Ken Maynard. And every kid was either a Tillicum, the club sponsored by the Vancouver *Province*, or of the one rather upstart nouveau Uncle Ben's Club, which was sponsored by the *Sun*. I was a loyal Tillicum. Membership in the Tillicums gave you a genuine imitation silver pin shaped like a totem and inscribed with "Kla Howya Tillicum". You got your name in the paper on your birthday.

It being wartime, everyone belonged to a gang. We were the Skull and Crossbones Gang and we drilled with fake guns and helmets. There was the Red, White and Blue Gang, too, and the dreaded Black Tigers who might sneak up at dawn on Sunday and wreck your clubhouse before daybreak. I still bear a scar from those titanic struggles. Bill Ritchie lobbed a hunk of firewood over a fence and split my skull, sending me screaming home to mommy with blood pouring down my face. As I recall I had four stitches and qualified, despite the panic bit, for the gang's equivalent of the Purple Heart. (Bill Ritchie and I remained good friends and later were fraternity brothers.)

When I grew up, the transit system was the streetcar, period. Going downtown from Macdonald and 41st Avenue you could take the Number 7 or 8—on the way back the Number 7 stopped at Dunbar while the Number 8 went down Dunbar to Broadway, I think. Tickets for kids, blue, were eight for a quarter while tickets for adults, yellow, they were four for a quarter. Every Friday the B.C. Electric, predecessor to B.C. Transit, put out their little newsletter with Reddy Kilowatt, who always had a corny joke.

There don't seem to be that many of us around. Real Vancouverites. You will meet lots who say "Well, I wasn't born in Vancouver but I've been here for 20 years ..." or "I came here when I was a child ..." or "I consider myself a Vancouver girl although ..." It's like a Scottish clan, you either are or you aren't. And I am. I was born in Vancouver on December 31, 1931, in Grace Hospital of a mother who was born here in 1906, twenty years after Vancouver got its charter. Her mother came on the first CPR passenger train, a native of Nova Scotia by name of Macdonald, which is almost as good as being a native Vancouverite.

How can you tell a native?

Easy. They say Kitsil*eye*no and Capil*eye*no and there is a "g" in Van*g*couver. And, no, they don't say "eh" all the time. That marks a Canadian (someone from east of the Rockies).

There is no way I can really make you believe the changes I have seen in Vancouver, the loveliest of all the world's cities. With the possible exception of Quebec and Montreal, this is the only Canadian city that's interesting.

Let me prove to you the changes that have taken place. When my mom was a girl the family summer home was at Jericho

Beach near where the Royal Vancouver Yacht Club now stands. Her family, the Leigh family, lived in the West End, as did the Mair family, who arrived from New Zealand in 1913. Mom and her family would take the streetcar to Broadway and Granville, where the hired man would pick them up with the wagon and take them to their summer place, now part of that long, long beach that starts at Kitsilano by the Burrard Street Bridge.

When I was a child, my grandparents on my mother's side had moved to a farm where they retired to raising chickens and growing cranberries. It was in Burnaby on Union Street. It took an hour to drive from our place in Kerrisdale through the east end of Vancouver, out past the "Technocracy" sign near the Royal Oak cemetery (where both my maternal grandparents now rest) through miles of open fields to the farm.

Vancouver was a city in the 1930s and 1940s, but it was a "rural" city and no matter where you lived, you were never far from the farm.

SCHOOL DAYS

I started school (after "graduating" from Jack and Jill Kindergarten at 45th and West Boulevard) at Maple Grove Elementary, which shared a school ground with Magee High School. (Actually my first schooling was at a kindergarten run by the Misses Beeman at 42nd and Macdonald. I enrolled myself after my pal Gregor MacIntosh—a grandson of Sir Richard McBride—was sent there and I missed him. My panic-stricken mother, thinking I'd been abducted, found me happily crayoning away with my new schoolmates!)

I remember much of my Maple Grove days. I recall being in love with Alice Pitcairn (as was every boy in the class) and later with Mary Ellen Taylor, for whose affection and on whose front lawn Richard Underhill, later a prominent Vancouver lawyer, and I wrestled. I well remember being chased with my pal and neighbour, Denis Hargrave, every day after school by Pat Higginbotham, who had a real two-wheel bicycle a year or so before the rest of us. That in itself scared the hell out of Denis and me. I remember my teachers, especially Miss Dunlop, Miss Shears and Miss Grey, all very kind ladies. Many years later I mentioned Miss Shears on air, saying that by this time she had undoubtedly gone to her reward and was horrified—and, of course, delighted—to get a call later from a very much alive Miss Shears. She had seemed so old when I went into Grade 1. She must have been at least as old as my mother!

Somehow you remember the stores from childhood. There was Couzens Drugs on the corner of 49th and West Boulevard where, if you were careful, you could pinch the odd comic book or Big Little Book, those wonderful little books that had pictures in the right-hand corner that turned into a sort of action movie if you quickly flipped the pages with your thumb. There was a little convenience store on 45th—probably around Larch—where we would buy the delicious Nickel Lunch, a sort of chocolate marshmallow delight, for a nickel, of course. And there was the Magee Grocery, which is still there.

I remember lots of the kids because I caught up with a few of them later in high school and many more at UBC. But I especially remember Michiko Katayama, a little Japanese girl I was kind of sweet on, who stopped coming to school in 1942 after she and her family were sent to an internment camp for the crime of being of Japanese origin. Her mom ran a bespoke hat store for ladies on West Boulevard until it was taken from her in 1942.

After Grade 4 my parents sent me to St. George's School for Boys where my pal Denis Hargrave had gone the year before. I went into Grade 5 but was moved up to Grade 6 after Christmas. I have mostly good memories of St. George's, which, in those days, was run like a British public school. Discipline was by the cane, wielded not only by masters but by senior boys called "prefects." It being wartime, the quality of teaching was considered low but I think that was wrong. If nothing else I learned a great love of British literature from a wonderful old guy named Captain B. O. Robinson, whose education was confined to what we would call high school. His initials always gave us much glee in those days of incessant ads that Lifebuoy Soap got rid of "Bee Ohhh" (body odour). Cappy, as we called him, had fits of violent temper because of a metal plate that had been inserted in his head courtesy of the First World War but we loved him—and he was a very fine teacher however minimal his formal training.

One anecdote about Captain Robinson. During the worst of the war—which we all followed with keen interest—Cappy constantly promised that when the war ended he would stand in front of the class and sing "When the Lights Go on Again (All

Over the World)." On May 8, 1945, he did just that.

I suppose because of my parents and attending St. George's, I was a keen follower of world events. In about Grade 7 I won the school prize for general knowledge. This interest—and hero worship of Winston Churchill—carried over into adulthood and to this day. At St. George's I was an Army Cadet—it was compulsory—but I also joined the Sea Cadets because I wanted to go to sea and serve in the navy.

The Sea Cadets, not to be confused with the Sea Scouts, were connected to the Royal Canadian Navy. When asked now how I remember so much about the war I answer, "because I was in the system." I learned to bayonet people and shoot straight so that, in a very few years' time, I would be ready to take my place. When you're twelve and thirteen this makes you think.

The Sea Cadets met and marched at the old roller skating pier that went into English Bay near the entrance to Stanley Park. It's long gone and forgotten now, but not by those who drilled there twice a week.

St. George's emphasized sports, especially rugby in the fall and winter months and cricket in the summer. I loved both games but was only moderately good at them. I especially loved cricket because my dad, as a Kiwi expatriate, played in the local league and I spent many pleasant afternoons at Brockton Point in Stanley Park watching him play. As an athlete I was always picked about third or fourth when teams were made up. Not terribly good but "useful," as the English put it so well. I got my "colours" for the Third XV and actually played a couple of games with the Second XV before moving to Prince of Wales in September 1946 for Grades 10 through 12.

I moved to Prince of Wales High School, which, with less than 200 kids, vied with University Hill as the smallest high school in Vancouver. A year or two before I arrived, the school district tried to close PW school, bringing an enormous demonstration from students and PW alumni alike. Mr. McCorkindale, the perpetual head of the school board, backed down. This was the same Mr. McCorkindale who kindly gave me permission to go to PW instead of Magee, my neighbourhood high school. Later I got to know his lovely daughter Mary, who married my childhood friend (and her childhood sweetheart) Gordon Christopher.

It wasn't that I had anything against Magee. It was just that through my cousins, Ann and Barbara Hatfield, I got to know so many kids from PW that I was hooked on the idea of going there. It was a decision I never regretted for a second. Because of its size, the students had tremendous school spirit. To this day when I meet an ex PW ite there is a special bond.

My writing career was launched at PW. I wrote a column called "Rattling Records with Rafe" in the *Three Feathers* newspaper (the Three Feathers being the crest of the Prince of Wales). In those days long before tapes and CDs, I wrote about the latest swing, boogie-woogie and bebop on wax. I learned a bit about "contra," for Thompson and Page in South Granville would, because I was a "record columnist," give me the odd free one. Helen Portinoff, a King Ed lass, worked the record desk and I got to listen to all the records I wanted for however long I wanted, not a bad perk for a kid in those days. I also seemed to write every other article for the 1949 Annual, my graduating year.

The second recollection is that my thespian career died a-borning at PW. I played the steward in "Our Hearts Were Young and Gay," a role with two lines, neither of which I could ever get down pat. To this day I can't memorize a thirty-second recording.

My wish to be with PW kids developed during the many happy summers I spent at Woodlands on the North Arm of Burrard Inlet, where my aunt and uncle, Bill and Lois Hatfield, owned a small island just offshore. Bill was a well-known internist whose name is still remembered in the medical fraternity. In addition to being my uncle, he was also my godfather though I don't remember too many talks with him on matters spiritual. I idolized my Uncle Bill and loved my Aunty Lo, who had a tremendous rapport with younger people. Their daughters were like my sisters and to this day Ann, now and for fifty years a Robertson, remains my big sister and one of my best pals.

The "Island," as we knew it, attracted young males like flies to honey mostly because Ann, then and now a beauty, had lots of beautiful girl friends. (Barby was also lovely and when her day came, the result was the same for that generation.) I was at an awkward age being three years younger than Ann but a couple of years older than Barby. For all that I tended to be allowed in with the "big kids" most of the time. Prominent among the "big kids" was Ann's future husband, Clark Robertson, who became a life-long friend of mine until his much and widely mourned death in 1999. I loved the Montreal Canadiens and he loved whom-ever they were playing; he in turn was a devout Notre Dame col-lege football fan and I always pulled for whomever happened to be on the other end of the gridiron from them. Clark was the best loved of men.

The "Island" had a saltwater pool filled by the higher of high tides that was the scene of hours of great fun for kids of all ages and lots of them. All were not just tolerated but truly loved by my Aunt Lo, though I suspect "tolerated" is the word Uncle Bill would have used to describe his feelings, especially when it came to the music. Those who have grown up listening to CDs or tapes cannot imagine what music sounded like with the old 78s on a wind-up gramophone! Yet Harry James with Helen Forrest singing Hoagy Carmichael's "Skylark" sounded so-o-o smooth to our ears. These were wonderful summers that none of us will ever forget.

Much of high school life in the 1940s revolved around movies and restaurant hangouts. I remember when the Vogue Theatre was built during the war. My mom and dad took me to the opening night, which I think was Noel Coward's wartime thriller *In Which We Serve* or maybe it was *This Happy Breed*. After the movie on Saturday we would repair to the Silk Hat on the cor-ner of Granville and I think it was Smithe, though it might have been Robson or Helmcken—it doesn't matter—it was on the northwest corner anyway and everyone had the fruit salad with the then-quite-novel soft ice cream.

There were a number of fashionable restaurants for west side kids in those days. In addition to the Silk Hat there were the 'Crats (Aristocratic Restaurants), one on the southwest corner of Broadway and Granville and on the northeast corner of 41st and Granville, where the Vancouver College kids in their draped yellow corduroy pants hung out. If you went to King Ed High School your hang-out was the Normandy near 12th and Granville. If you went to PW, it was the Blue Boy at 15th and Granville, run by a Mrs. Littler. We called it "Littler's Lousy Lunch." Actually Mrs. Littler was very nice and you could get a decent sandwich and a Coke for a quarter and another quarter gave you six plays in the jukebox. How the hell she got by on what we spent in there is beyond me, especially after we learned in chemistry that if you put a penny into sulphuric acid you could reduce it to the size of a dime and thus get two of Tommy Dorsey's latest out of the Wurlitzer for a slightly amended penny. (The jig was up when, as school treasurer, I had to explain to the teacher I reported to, Russ Robinson, how the Coke machine in my charge was full of shiny, very thin one-cent pieces. For awhile it was a helluva deal, for Cokes only cost seven cents, meaning that for a fake dime you got a Coke plus three more potential "dimes.")

Virginity was a little more difficult to lose back then because this was before the pill. I managed to lose mine at sixteen anyway. What a horrible and sudden outburst that was. But it did get me launched, so to speak, and with experience came better control. But parents, who were remarkably loath to discuss the finer points of sex, worried deeply about daughters getting pregnant and sons being prematurely fathers. And so they should have. In the mid-1940s bolder parents took their kids to see a movie called *Mom and Dad*. It was a ghastly display of horror stories designed to make sex seem so repulsive that no one would want to try it. This was supposed to take the place of the "sex talk" that most parents dreaded. Audiences were segregated, with boys at one showing and girls at another.

Those were different days in many ways. Halloween was a hellish night. Kids burned everything they couldn't tip over and the police had their hands full. When I hear my contemporaries complain about the kids today I shake my head as I hearken back to those days mercifully behind us.

But for all that they were pretty safe days. Everyone hitch-hiked—girls, too—and there were never any problems. And no one locked anything, least of all the front door.

I look back on my school days with almost undiluted pleasure. I was a very lucky kid and was especially lucky to wind up with friends and acquaintances from three different schools, who all came together at university and in later life.

WHITHER RADIO?

It's interesting to speculate where radio is headed. After the Second World War, when television was just getting going, the futurists all predicted the end of radio. Television would take over. After all, who wanted to listen when you could both listen and watch? Yet radio not only survived, it prospered.

Part of radio's endurance is built in. You can't drive a car, read a book or ogle a member of the opposite sex to the accompaniment of television. Moreover television is prohibitively expensive to produce, which no doubt accounts for the fact that while I have nearly 175 channels on my cable service, I have a hell of a time finding anything to watch for the half hour a day I spare television as I do my treadmill exercises. When it comes to news, it's perhaps a toss-up. Unless the event is predictable, such as the wars in the Balkans or in Afghanistan, radio gets there first. The later television coverage is perhaps sexier but, again, that's a set piece and a very expensive exercise.

Looking ahead at radio in Vancouver, the Canadian hotbed of open line radio, makes me pretty pessimistic at three score and ten. That's because radio in Vancouver shows all the signs of going the way the print media has gone.

I was dismayed, in December 2001, when I had four young people on my show from the B.C. Youth Parliament. Apart from the young lady from the Alliance, I didn't hear a spark of anger at the system that now envelopes this country and the dismal inheritance that is theirs.

We have become corporatized, in government and in the media. As a starting point I go back to the Charlottetown

Referendum in 1992. For what was so obviously a badly flawed document that it would have done irreparable harm, Prime Minister Mulroney obtained support from every aspect of the Canadian establishment—the political parties, the business community, the labour unions, the artsy fartsy crowd and, yes, the media. In fact the real point of that exercise came when Maclean-Hunter, the major media outlet, formally signed on with the Yes Committee. Without belabouring the point it came as a huge surprise to the local Southam-controlled press when British Columbia massively rejected the deal, so out of touch were they. A couple of years later, Southam took three prominent writers off the Kemano II controversy because they had asked uncomfortable questions of Alcan, a major advertiser. As a billion dollar hydro deal was brought to its heels you would never have known that there was a controversy by reading the local press.

There is, you see, an undefined but very real limit on dissent in this country and it is getting more limited and better defined.

Daniel Webster once said, "The contest for ages has been to rescue liberty from the grasp of executive power." We have now got total executive power in this country. The need for hellraising has never been greater. We have a constitution constipated with vetoes at a time when our instruments of government have been taken over by the command section of the prime minister's office, with MPs truly, in Trudeau's term, nobodies. Never has the voter felt so disconnected from those who sit in the parliaments and legislatures of the land. It isn't a question of giving voice to those who are right but to those who question and do so in clear and perhaps even pungent tones.

And what do we have? A media getting more pallid, more anonymous, more obsequious by the day. Most of the print media in this country and, with the exception of the always gutsy *Georgia Straight*, all of the Vancouver media, are controlled by Izzy Asper through his son Leonard. When the *National Post* got too close to the bone with the Shawinigan scandal involving

Izzy's pal and political soulmate Jean Chrétien, they were defanged. The orders, I am reliably informed, went out in 2001 that no editorials or op-ed pieces in Asper newspapers or on his Global TV are to criticize the state of Israel. Indeed, these media outlets must report Middle East news putting Israel in a favourable light. In June of 2002, the Aspers tried to get CKNW to get me to "pipe down" by withholding advertising and ending all joint ventures. Fortunately, CKNW is a rarity and supported me fully.

Does this spill over into commentators and columnists? It must. All must eat and support families. Moreover, the Aspers of the world hire people of their views to avoid the charge that they are manipulating opinion in this country.

It doesn't mean that there cannot be courageous pieces. They just can't be critical of the government or Israel. Some writers may try to push at the boundaries but, for the most part, the print media's rage is directed at targets acceptable to the publishers.

What about radio? And what about radio here in Vancouver, where there is a long tradition of feistiness and irreverence toward authority?

I can only express my fears. The leading station, over the years, has been CKNW with Webster and Bannerman and, in earlier days, CJOR with Pat Burns. CJOR now plays nostalgic music and CKNW has fallen into the corporate hands of Bay Street and Wall Street. It remains to be seen what will happen.

At this writing I'm still bellowing my outrage every morning but where's the bull pen? CKNW sacked the one ray of light for those who like candid radio—Shiral Tobin. Too inexperienced, they said; I say, too gutsy and, worst of all, female. Where are the hellraisers of tomorrow? Who will ask hard questions the next time the government gets the entire establishment behind a bad deal as happened with the Charlottetown Accord? Who will take on big business and big labour? There will always be broadcasters who will, in a "on the one hand, on the other hand" sort of way, ask questions. But who will stand against what they think is wrong with all the strength they can summon up?

My fear for CKNW is that it is going to be, once I'm out of the way, just another radio station. Safe, mildly controversial at best, all broadcasters will be carefully selected as people who will not ruffle corporate accounts, actual or prospective. They will treat those who govern us with gentle nudges at most. The arrival of infomercials, and the management going to bean counters, surely points the way. It isn't a case of whether or not a Pat Burns, Jack Webster or Rafe Mair is permitted on the air but will they be actively recruited as in the past?

Let me tell you a story to illustrate. I left CJOR in 1984, after getting second prize in a contract dispute. Ted Smith, then general manager of CKNW, hired me to do a new show from midnight until two in the morning. I was scarcely a crucial part of their broadcasting day or a key member of their team. On one of my very first broadcasts I said to a caller, "I ate a McDonald's hamburger about eight years ago and to this day, when I burp, I can taste the damned thing." Not especially bright or witty but there it was.

McDonald's set its hair on fire and demanded that I be taken off the air. Ted Smith politely but firmly told them to go to hell, that CKNW stood behind their broadcasters. They always have and I can tell you it hasn't always been easy. Most importantly, they have stood behind them when the majority thought they were wrong and when they were in fact wrong.

I look back at the times when Bill Vander Zalm was premier and half the province was complaining about my editorials. Then manager Ron Bremner never flinched. I can only imagine what it must have been like when the prime minister on down was bashing at management over my position on the Charlottetown Accord and the heat they took from Alcan during the Kemano II struggle.

Is management up to this any more? Is it in the corporate interest to have broadcasters fire shots at will? Or will we be seeing potential advertisers featured guests on air as part of the advertising package? I don't know. I have to hope for the best.

My time is passing. Not much is left to separate free speech and courageous journalism on the one hand and, if I may coin a phrase, the corporatization of Canada. It's not, as I hope I have demonstrated, a new thing but it has been growing steadily. The new motto is "Dissent if you will, but always be polite and don't ever get too close to the bone. And when push comes to shove, your company, your union and especially your government is probably right. Best to go along."

The evidence is there for all to see. We are more and more being treated as a nation of wimps by those who are set in authority over us. The day is not far off, I fear, when the process will be complete and the media will be merely organs of the establishment.

British Columbians ... Canadians ... should think about this before it's too late.

MUSIC AND THE SAVAGE BREAST

William Congreve, who among other things claimed the daughter of the first Duke of Marlborough as his mistress, said, "Music hath charms to soothe the savage breast, to soften rocks, or bend a knotted oak."

My relationship with music is better summed up, I think, by the great English conductor, Sir Thomas Beecham, who said, "The English hate music but they love the noise it makes."

I love music and the noise it makes and my tastes are eclectic to say the least. I grew up in the swing era and the beginnings of bebop and, to this day, love to put on Glen Miller or one of the old Jazz at the Philharmonic CDs that have been so brilliantly remastered.

My problem was the early days of rock, which came upon me in my early twenties. Actually, the predecessor to rock, called "race," was well within my time and was epitomized by such artists as Louis Jordan and Wynonie Harris. Though I have since come to like them and respect their talents, I just didn't dig Elvis, The Big Bopper, Jerry Lee Lewis and Buddy Holly. It's funny, though, some of the music I hated came onto me later in life. In retrospect, I like Ricky Nelson, especially "Hello Mary Lou," and have become quite fond of the Beatles. I saw the musical *Buddy* in London and thoroughly enjoyed it. The Beatles and the rest of the electric guitar freaks seemed to me to just be a lot of bloody noise. But this was the music of my children and aren't parents supposed to hate their children's music? Mine detested the music of my era, especially the fads such as Frankie Laine (who in fact, before they made him into a cowboy, was a very fine jazz singer as his album with Buck Clayton, recently re-issued on CD, will attest), Johnny Ray and company. For all generations, the music in the "Easy Listening" bin now is the music that your parents told you you'd go to hell in a handcart for listening to when it was popular. Seeing Elvis in that bin now is proof positive of that for me.

During the 1960s, 1970s and to some extent the 1980s I needed something to listen to. Although singers such as Tom Jones and Engelbert Humperdinck were eminently listenable, so was Cyndi Lauper for that matter. Nat "King" Cole was still there. King Cole was unquestionably the greatest popular music performer of the twentieth century. Others could sing, some could play and a few could be counted on to break new ground. Cole did all of that and more. An all-star jazz pianist from whose musical loins George Shearing sprang, Nat neatly survived and indeed made commercial crap sound good. I once asked Frankie Laine who was the biggest influence on his life and wasn't surprised to hear him say Nat "King" Cole. Thirty-five years after his death he still sells ten million records a year!

Throughout the 1970s I felt the need to relate to something new, yet not noisy rubbish, which is what I thought of the music of the time. The Poppy Family—Terry and Susan Jacks—filled the bill for me because they were singing about contemporary issues ("six months in jail for just smokin' pot") and were clearly good musicians. Much more popular, of course, and great favourites of mine were Simon and Garfunkel. To this day I will stop what I'm doing to hear "Bridge Over Troubled Water" from start to finish, a daunting task if you're busy. The Manhattan Transfer did it for me, too, and so did the Everly Brothers, though they weren't particularly good musicians, as did the Beatles. I really liked the Mamas and the Papas and "Crique Alley" remains a great favourite, as does, of course, Mama Cass Elliot singing "Dream a Little Dream of Me." (Do you remember the horrible quip, "If Karen Carpenter had eaten the sandwich that Mama Cass choked on they'd both be alive today"?)

I have always been partial to singing groups and I suppose my all-time favourites, whom I saw several times in the flesh, were the Mills Brothers. They continued to be popular until death broke them up in the 1980s.

I loved (and continue to love) Jo Stafford, June Christy, Helen O'Connell, Anita O'Day, Billie Holiday, Sarah Vaughn and, most especially Ella (like Louis, Sarah, Miles and Oscar, no surname is necessary). But the woman who saved the musical lives of so many stuck in my time warp, Barbra Streisand, did and does nothing for me (she shouts). Diana Krall from Nanaimo is simply great.

The 1980s and 1990s would have been pretty tough years had it not been for ABBA. They were simply fantastic and in my car's twelve-CD holder there is always one ABBA and one Nat "King" Cole. But I find I enjoy classical music in the car in preference to anything else.

I have found, in later years, that I love much classical music. Not all by any means. I'm not big on Gregorian chants for one thing. And I like opera music but not the operas themselves. They're too damned long for one thing. I have the attention span of a gnat, and when anything lasts more than two hours it loses me, no matter how noisy it might be. A few years ago my wife and I started going to the opera to patronize the arts and be seen by the very best people. It was *The Barber of Seville* and the bloody thing went nearly four hours. It looked to me like a dozen or more Mr. Beans (whom I detest) set to music. I swore off attending opera performances, though I continue to listen to a number of CDs with opera music, especially the overtures.

My mother loved the classics. Though scarcely a music snob—her absolute, all time favourite was Bing Crosby singing "Stardust" though I suspect that this had less to do with Der Bingle than a love affair recalled—she went to the symphony regularly and played her music on our old gramophone. I remember some of her favourites. Beethoven's "Appassionata" sonata and his Fifth Symphony, Tchaikovsky's famous Piano

Concerto No. 1 in B-Flat Minor, Ravel's "Bolero," Bizet's *Carmen* and anything by Chopin and Grieg.

I learned to love these pieces and Strauss waltzes as well.

"Real" music lovers seemed to reject some pieces as "too modern" or on some other artificial basis and I found myself unwilling to expose my bad taste by saying that one of my favourite pieces of music was Strauss' "Tales from the Vienna Woods."

I went to school with Frederick C. Clarke, who went on to greater things on the Canadian music scene—I'm not quite sure what but I know he went to Toronto and is listed as author of a number of hymns in the Anglican hymn book, which is good enough for me. In any event, as the boy musical genius of my pre-youth, he pooh-poohed the Strausses and held that Tchaikovsky was too modern to be taken seriously. Because popular music didn't quite have the priesthood of classical music, I listened to the big bands, boogie-woogie and the great singers that the 1930s spawned.

Now I wish I'd been less sensitive and listened to more classical music. I have perhaps 100 classical music CDs—more like 300 of other stuff—and enjoy them immensely. But I know nothing about the classics that would get me past the kindergarten of music. And that I regret.

What I do find is that as I spend time in CD stores I look more and more at the classics section. And I buy classical music almost exclusively. And I'm learning every day.

Especially when you reach the "grumpy old man" age learning every day is what makes life worth living, isn't it?

ON FISHING AND OTHER SPORTS

Why Are We Fans?

I've often wondered what it is in the human psyche that makes us fans of sports teams, loyal to our favourite sports hero. I can understand loyalty to one's family. That's likely some primitive traditional need, inherited rather than learned. Loyalty to one's country, whether inherited or not, makes sense for reasons of preservation of culture, prosperity and safety from the nation's enemies. Loyalty is a very strong emotion, otherwise why would people be willing to die for their country? What I find more difficult to understand is loyalty to an athlete or sports team.

When I was much younger, I was a devout Montreal Canadiens fan. Why?

Even though I couldn't skate and had never been to Montreal, I not only loved the team with passion but with even greater passion I hated their opponents, the Toronto Maple Leafs. Why?

My loyalty was so strong that if a Leafs player was traded to the Canadiens, as were Dick Duff, Gaye Stewart and Frank Mahovolich, I thought the bastards would go easy on the Leafs and could never really accept them as true Canadiens. (Come to think of it, this is probably why I don't follow team sports much any more—the players are traded far too often. Hell, you can't even keep track of where the teams have moved these days.)

My sole remaining sports loyalty is to Tiger Woods. When he's playing, I play every shot with him. When he three-putted the fifteenth on the last day of the 2001 Masters, I didn't know whether to cry or curse, so I did both.

Is it because we see ourselves in our heroes' shoes, like a latter-day Walter Mitty—the James Thurber character who daydreamed himself into heroic roles, most amusingly played by Danny Kaye in *The Secret Life of Walter Mitty* (1947)? That must be it because when Tiger wins, I feel that all who know me should congratulate me. Do we cheer for an athlete or a sports team not because we somehow feel connected to them but because they fill a void of accomplishment in our own lives? Am I walking down the eighteenth at Augusta with Tiger because I could never get there on my own? Do I take his losses personally because I believe that personally I've been hurt, probably unfairly?

Perhaps a more important question is how we translate our fandom from merely loving a golfer or sports franchise full of highly paid performers into questions of a nationalistic imperative. Would anyone, the morning after the 2002 Olympic hockey win over the U.S.A. dare admit they hadn't seen the game from start to finish? Why on earth was this game so important?

An interesting place, Canada. Before the 2002 Olympic wins by both the men's and women's hockey teams, our other defining moment was the eighth and last game of the 1972 Canada-Russia hockey series. Everybody in the country watched and I managed to put aside the uncomfortable and annoying if not unfair fact that Paul Henderson, a Toronto Maple Leaf, scored the winning goal. I consoled myself with the thought that Montreal Canadien Yvan Cournoyer tied the game and then went on to set up Paul Henderson's goal. The men's Olympics final on February 24, 2002, was another defining moment. Had we lost, presumably we would have taken to the streets and rioted as Vancouver fans did the night they lost the Stanley Cup final in 1994. Chest thumping after a win and rioting after a loss seem to be in the national character.

Like all Canadians, I was glued to my television set during the men's Olympic hockey finals and there were tears in my eyes when they played "O Canada" to honour us and our team. Nothing that follows is intended to detract one iota from what was a most deserved victory and a great moment for every Canadian.

But I couldn't help thinking that our government spends

hundreds of millions of tax dollars each year telling us what a great country we are. When a cabinet minister, John Manley, makes the obvious observation that we have fallen far behind the United States in standard of living, his colleague, Sheila Copps, feels the need to instantly rebut the obvious—she being the same person who spent a minimum of $25 million—many retailers think it was more—on Canadian flags in 1996.

On the eve of the Charlottetown Referendum, now nearly ten years ago, Prime Minister Mulroney opined that the Referendum would no doubt go well for him because the Toronto Blue Jays had just won the World Series!

And perhaps that's the point. We are indeed together emotionally during these sports teams wins. The emotional bond overrides the lack of political commonality, even I dare say, in Quebec. We come together and seize upon the winning of even a bronze medal at an athletic meet as a sign of great national accomplishment, yet we can't agree on a common Canadian history for school kids. We honour athletes and sports teams yet squabble like alley cats over whether or not a certain prime minister, Trudeau comes to mind, was a great man or the worst thing to ever happen to the country.

I'm not suggesting that pride in athletes or sports teams is a bad thing. But other countries don't resort to fandom as a means of convincing themselves that they really are a united country and all love one another deep down. They love to win—indeed so much when they do but they have a self-confidence and, unlike Canadians, are not surprised at themselves but proud when they win.

After 135 years of existence Canadians still are not convinced that Canada is a real country. And perhaps we're not. We had a funny beginning. Canada didn't come into being because of an association so long that any other conclusion was unthinkable. The original marriage on July 1, 1867, was seen in Halifax as a tawdry shotgun affair, such that merchants hung black crepe in their windows. Indeed countries with backgrounds similar to ours often still have serious internal conflict. Britain and Spain forced confederation on independent states and continue with civil strife today, the majority usually relying on historical strife to reinforce their position.

Canada had no defining war, only the threat of takeover from the United States. That threat has not convinced us of our Canadian nationality. The United States, as were most countries, was conceived, born and ripened in fire. Their constitution was a well thought-out answer to other methods of governance. When the meaning of their constitution, namely the respective powers of the federal government and the states, was forced to the front by the issue of slavery, it was settled by what was to that time the bloodiest war in history.

It is not my case that we should have a war in Canada or that even one stone should be thrown in anger. It is to say that if we want to be more than a conglomeration of disparate individuals and regions that come together from time to time to cheer on an athlete or sports team, we would be wise to go through a serious and protracted period of introspection.

Let's deal with the question of an accepted national history. Why is it that we can't come up with something that we can all buy into? Traditionally, Canadian histories have been written from an eastern perspective, with the history of its outer regions considered as appendages. For example, about five years ago I was inspired to write a book because I could not find out who the first premier of British Columbia was in any of the standard texts, very much including the text considered the Canadian Bible in some places, A. R. M. Lower's *Colony to Nation: The Story of Canada* (Longmans, 1947, reprinted McClelland & Stewart, 1977). I was astonished to interview a well-known Canadian author who had written that our first premier was Amor de Cosmos. She refused to accept my assurance that she was wrong. The first premier of British Columbia, John Foster McCreight, was not a notable person but that's not the point. The point is that in the accepted versions of Canadian history, written and published in Toronto, a Canadian, including the writer I interviewed, could not research the point.

I also submit that one of the reasons British Columbians specifically and Canadians generally have been unable to come to grips with aboriginal issues in British Columbia is that all we were taught about were Iroquois, Huron and Algonquin and nothing about Musqueam, Haida and Shuswap.

In short, two points. First, a country ignorant about itself or, even worse, with an establishment-accepted history that skews facts to suit the desires of one region of the country, no matter how important that region may be, cannot be united. Second, a country that does not have a system of governance, never mind how well or badly it works, that does not satisfy the needs of its people and regions will never be a nation.

A country does not need a founding revolution followed by a bloody civil war to become a nation. But it is necessary to spend a great deal of time and real effort making up for those two deficiencies by constantly reviewing how we govern ourselves and paying real attention to those people and regions who feel badly done by. It's because we haven't and now have no national will to do so that our national pride depends so much on the outcome of a game of shinny played by youthful millionaires.

A LOOK BACK AT BASEBALL

Well, it isn't quite like making the Hall of Fame but Wendy and I have shared a bit of baseball history. We saw one of Barry Bonds' record-breaking home runs in April 2001 against the Cincinnati Reds, a game that also, to the great glee of the fans, saw Ken Griffey Jr. strike out with the bases loaded. Both moments went all for naught as the Reds won the game.

I thought of how much the game has changed since I was a boy sitting in the bleachers of Capilano Stadium, back in the 1946 sunshine, watching the old Class B Capilanos playing against Spokane or Tri Cities or Victoria, when the only thing that mattered was that there was lots of Cracker Jack and that the home team won.

We didn't really notice it then, because we were used to nothing else, but it was a white man's game and, of course, all the records were white men's records.

I used to think that Lou Gehrig's record of 2,130 straight games, Ty Cobb's lifetime hits and Babe Ruth's 60 homers in a season were unassailable. Now all three records have not only been beaten, they've been shattered in the same way that hockey records have been shattered. And golf's. And football's. As the saying goes, "Records are made to be broken."

In baseball, the playing conditions have improved, the equipment is better and the players are bigger, stronger by far and in much better shape. George Herman "Babe" Ruth would have found it tough making the Yankees today because he just wouldn't be able to move that beer belly far enough in the outfield. He could be the designated hitter, of course, an abomination that has changed the game for the worse. The strategy of baseball when you have a pitcher hitting compared with when you don't (as in the American League with its panty-waist designated hitter rule) is dramatic. That's one big change.

The biggest change by far, though, happened in 1947 when, after leading the Triple A International League in hitting, one Jack Roosevelt Robinson opened the season at first base with the Brooklyn Dodgers. He was the first black to play modern "organized" baseball, a euphemism for the whiteness of the game until then. We now recognize that the Negro Leagues played major league ball, too. We affirm that fact with a special category for blacks from those leagues to enter the Hall of Fame in Cooperstown, New York. That place, incidentally, has dick-all to do with baseball and neither did Abner Doubleday, but that's another story.

Back in 1961, when Roger Maris beat Babe Ruth's home run record with 61, then Commissioner Ford Frick decreed that an asterisk appear next to the number in the record book because Maris had a dozen or so more games in which to do it. I think an asterisk should appear on all records compiled before, say, 1960, when a fair complement of blacks finally played the game. Would Joe DiMaggio have hit in 56 consecutive games had he faced the great black pitchers of the game such as Satchel Paige?

Come to think of it, given the rise to prominence of Japanese players, with Ichiro Suzuki winning the American League Batting championship in 2001, there may be the need for yet another asterisk to mark the long era that Americans have considered Japanese ball players to be inferior.

It wasn't only blacks who had a hard time getting to play "organized" ball. Recently, a wonderful video was released, *The Life and Times of Hank Greenberg* (1999), which tells the great baseball story of the great Detroit Tiger who led his team to four World Series and two World Series rings. But for nearly four seasons lost in Army service—he was drafted in the peacetime draft of 1940 and didn't return until July 1945 when he helped the

Tigers to a pennant and a World Series win over the Chicago Cubs—Greenberg would have been up there with Aaron, Ruth and Bonds for all-time homers.

In Greenberg's first game back after four years, he hit a homer. By pre-arrangement all his teammates ignored him when he came back to the dugout. Greenberg, perplexed, went to the water cooler to get a drink, whereupon all his teammates leapt to their feet, swarmed him, patted his back and screamed their approval and "welcome back."

But Hank's story is a social one, too, for he was the first Jewish baseball star and put up with much the same viciousness on that account as Jackie Robinson did because he was black.

After Greenberg was traded to the Pittsburgh Pirates in 1947, he and Robinson played against each other. When Robinson ran over top of Greenberg at first base one day Greenberg helped the young black rookie to his feet and told him that he was not only a fine ballplayer but a fine young man. This from a man whose teammate "Dixie" Walker had been traded to the Pirates from the Dodgers because he didn't want to play with a "nigra."

Robinson responded by telling the press, "Mr. Greenberg is a great player and a class act."

Thus did Jew meet Black and, thank God, the game has never been the same since.

THE ROCKET

Perhaps a final word on Maurice "The Rocket" Richard would be in order, given the huge and emotional send-off he received in Montreal from Canadians of all ethnic backgrounds when he died in May 2001. I saw Richard play only twice, once in an exhibition game in about 1947 played at Queen's Park Arena in New Westminster, and once in an exhibition game of old-timers to open the new Pacific Coliseum in 1967. Richard scored a goal in the first game and I, a teenager, was thrilled to get his autograph. In the second game The Rocket didn't score. He did get sent in on a breakaway, though, and the goaltender, I think it was Sawchuk, stoned him, whereupon Richard broke his stick on the ice in anger. And that spoke volumes. It was only an old-timers' exhibition, yet he hated himself for failing.

Much has been written about the St. Patrick's Day riot in 1955 and how that galvanized the Quebeckers, and it undoubtedly did. What is astonishing is that English-speaking Canada, so vociferously critical of Richard for sparking that riot, now looks back on him, in death, in almost heroic terms.

A few years back I was privileged to have The Rocket in my studio. Unquestionably, everyone at the studio knew they were in the presence of an extraordinary man.

Richard's scoring prowess was considerable, such that Bill Chadwick, then Chief Referee in the National Hockey League, admitted in an article in *Maclean's* magazine that referees gave opposing players liberties handling Richard, otherwise he could not be stopped. Happily that logic didn't apply by the time Phil Esposito and Wayne Gretzky came along.

In the ancient argument about which player was better, Richard or Gordie Howe, most hockey buffs chose Howe. Not me. I supported Maurice Richard every time and I'll tell you why. It's undeniable that Howe outscored Richard, though not game for game during the time both men were playing. Howe was less fragile, having sustained only one serious injury in his long career. And he was a great player. But I take Richard on two points which I think are beyond debate.

First, when it came to the big goal, especially in Stanley Cup play and even more especially in overtime, Maurice Richard was the man everyone wanted on the ice.

Second, he was a leader. With Gordie Howe, the Red Wings won five straight league titles, yet they won the Stanley Cup only twice in that time. In the five-year stretch right afterward, the Canadiens won the league title four times (the other they were second to Detroit) and won the Cup all five times with The Rocket as captain. In all, Richard won eight Stanley Cups.

This is not to derogate from Howe's magnificent record. It is only to say that, during the days when the Red Wings were great, Ted Lindsay and Red Kelly were the leaders, not Howe.

But all that doesn't really matter. What does matter is how Richard was regarded as a man. Any who saw the closing of the old Montreal Forum in March 1996 will never forget the twelve-minute standing ovation Richard got—and that nearly forty years after he'd played his last game. Any who watched the proceedings during the week leading up to his funeral could not help but feel the very special place this man held in the hearts of all Canadians.

Maurice Richard went out as he played the game of hockey and the game of life—with pride and class.

Adieu, ami, adieu.

HOLD THAT TIGER!

Eldrick "Tiger" Woods perhaps, at twenty-six, is already the greatest golfer of all time. That, I suppose, remains to be proved over his entire career but no one would deny his extraordinary talent. His attempt to overhaul Jack Nicklaus' record of eighteen major tournaments may ironically be beyond reach because of the infinitely better competition Tiger will face from the upcoming golfers he has inspired.

Golf is a very difficult game, an "umbling" game it is often said.

One part of golf is seldom mentioned, yet in my opinion it is the most important of all. As the legendary Bobby Jones said, "Competitive golf is played mainly on a five-and-a-half-inch course, the space between your ears." The mental approach to golf isn't just having the smarts to play a golf course—to know when to gamble and when to play safe. That's incredibly important but there's more. It's called "heart"—the ability to stay cool when things aren't going well—which in this game is very often indeed. Some golfers are winners and some aren't. You see that at the club level and on the Professional Golfers' Association tour. The winners are the ones who apparently let nothing faze them and come right back with success after failure. These are guys who can follow a triple bogie with three straight birdies.

No golfer has this part of the game more under control than Tiger Woods, so well exemplified at the 2000 PGA. You may remember that he won in a play-off with a journeyman player named Bob May.

The eighteenth hole (seventy-second of the tournament), was a par five. After three shots, May was at the back, off the green and about fifty feet away with a slippery, downhill slider, Woods was about five feet away. Over hill, over dale went May's putt and in it went! As a former low handicapper I can tell you that shakes you. Not only did Woods now have a five footer to tie, it was the putt that every right-hander hates—left to right and down hill. This is the putt for which you either overcompensate and pull or hit too gently to have it slide away to the right. Woods went through his usual motions, stepped up and holed the putt. Not a big deal? Try it under that kind of pressure.

After Woods won the play-off he was asked about the situation in which he found himself after May had drained his overlander.

Woods said, "I had a feeling he was going to sink it. When he did, I just put myself in the present and hit my putt."

"I just put myself in the present." What a thought! What a message! How many of us, in whatever happens to us in life, can "put ourselves in the present"? Tiger doesn't mean blocking out the past, that's too risky. To put yourself in the present means that the past is irrelevant to what you must now do and cannot take up even one teeny little brain cell. There is no time for thinking about a missed putt a few holes before. There is no time to moan or to marvel at what your opponent has done, how bloody lucky Tiger was and how unfair it all is. No, you must deal with but one thing at the present moment—sinking a very tough putt.

In all likelihood I won't be around when Tiger finishes his career. But I hope to see as much of it as I can. And no matter how wonderfully he plays, no matter how long the drive, how close the iron shot or how amazing the recovery, I will always remember Tiger Woods for one ability—he can put himself "in the present." It is that which sets him apart from the rest of us on or off the golf course.

THE RIGHT TO FLY-FISH

I suspect that, though happily not in my lifetime, sports fishing will either be banned or made so uncomfortable that it might as well be. That statement might seem strange in light of the huge boom in the industry—especially in fly-fishing—but I suspect that this is the calm before the storm.

Fly-fishing has a long history. It is thought that the ancient Macedonians fished with a fly. Certainly the Romans did. Dame Juliana Berners, an abbess, wrote of it in the sixteenth century and many of the fly patterns she wrote of are still in use today, if in a somewhat altered form. Isaak Walton most famously wrote on the subject in the seventeenth century and *The Compleat Angler* (1653) tells less about how to catch fish than what it means to commune with nature and live with life as its being acted out. Walton did more—he spawned a literature about fishing that includes such authors as Guy de Maupassant, Ernest Hemingway, Zane Grey, G. E. M. Skues, Theodore Gordon and, probably the best of them all, Roderick Haig-Brown, who spent most of his adult life in Campbell River, British Columbia. To this day you will find the most elegant of writing among fly-fishers such as Ernest Schwiebert, Robert Traver, David Profumo and Nick Lyons. I tell you all this because, to millions through the ages, fishing is about more than catching fish. It's more than a pastime or a hobby, too. For those of us who tie our own flies, lost in dreams of where these will be used, mingled with reveries of past successes, fishing is an all-consuming passion.

Fishing has its victim, of course: the fish. Let that be stated front and centre. Even anglers who catch and release are tormenting the fish. And here is where the action starts, for the British Parliament has banned fox hunting, not on the basis that the fox dies, but on the ground that the sport is cruel. On this ground those who love fly-fishing are forced to take a stand. Because, although I think hounding foxes is as cruel as it can get, I recognize that the foxhunter and I are comrades-in-arms. Perhaps the opening shot ought to be a solid ad hominem attack on our tormentors by reminding them of Lord Thomas Macaulay's aphorism, "The Puritan hated bear-baiting, not because it gave pain to the bear, but because it gave pleasure to the spectators." The anti-hunter, you see, cares not a fig for the animal he seeks to protect. If he did he would be after others who are that animal's mortal enemy. Nature is cruel. The deer is not dealt with in gentlemanly fashion by the wolf nor the rabbit by the eagle. No, the anti-hunter is not upset at the cruel end suffered by any of the animals he or she protects but by the fact that hunters derive pleasure from the hunt. Indeed, the anti-hunter is indifferent to the fact that the farmer, no longer defended by the hunt, will have to poison or trap foxes just as our governments will have to do the same to wolves and coyotes. It's that fellow humans dress up and make the chase that's so dreadful.

Now I admit that it's no excuse to behave badly because others do the same. But having said that, let me observe that the leather on our feet and the steak on our table are acquired with a far greater cruelty than that inflicted on the venison. And fish, caught by the angler are, if kept, quickly dispatched while those taken in the commercial fishery are permitted to slowly suffocate to death.

It's a cruel world out there. And it may well be that humanity's next great undertaking ought to be the banning of cruelty wherever it's found. The easier targets for this great crusade are those who care far more about the environment within which their prey lives than those who practise condominium conservationism and, unwilling and unable to do anything at all about the truly great issues of worldwide cruelty, target me at my fly-tying vise.

WHAT'S A FLY?

Some fly-tying patterns placed before this aging fly-fisherman by the best of fly-fishing magazines are simply not flies. I don't know why they aren't but, dammit, they're not. The question has become, what is fly-fishing and what is not?

Over the years of practising the pleasures of fly-fishing and fly-tying I have developed, in the back of my mind, some doubts as to what fly-fishing is and what constitutes a fly.

I first fished with a fly in 1942 at the famous lake in the British Columbia Interior, Lac Lejeune, with my father and one of his best friends, "Uncle" Med. In those days the flies used were often English flies like the Dusty Miller, the Black Gnat and the fly they once tried to ban because it was so deadly, the Alexandra. Mingled in the fashionable fly-box of that era were patterns by the well-known Paul Lake guide, Bill Nation. If one were to compare that fly-box to the modern one, the conclusion would be that in days of yore flies weren't meant to look much like anything a trout might encounter on his constant search for food. But the old flies worked—and I often wonder how well they would work today. Do fish learn to look down their noses at a Black O'Lindsay, or a Nation's Special and insist upon a Shaw's Mayfly Nymph or Brian Chan's Red Assed Chironomid, both at least impressionistic representatives of the real critter?

What was a fly thirty years ago when I started to tie with some seriousness? There were, roughly, three main categories—dry, that is to say, surface flies; wet, that is to say, winged flies that sank; and nymphs. These subdivided into three overlapping categories, those that simply attracted, those that gave the impression of an aquatic dweller and those that would have the real thing trying to mate with them. Some wet flies—those for Atlantic salmon especially—distinctly did not imitate food forms since their quarry didn't feed on anything in the places they were used. Some wet flies were, it was supposed, representative of an emerging insect. Nymphs ranged all the way from an imitation of only one food source to offerings that fish might take because they look like a number of new foods.

Dries were interesting. If one is to believe the literature out of the New York Catskills, where the famous Beaverkill and Neversink Rivers run, the dry fly presented to imitate a hatch simply had to be a Hendrickson not a Quill Gordon and then it had to be perfectly constructed with all the proper ingredients and just the right size. (One popular English fly, the Tup's Indispensable, has a body of yellow wool and, according to those who know these things, that wool must be urine stained wool from a ram's testicular region.)

On western waters, somehow the fish weren't so selective and such imprecise offerings like the Humpy or the Tom Thumb seemed to do just fine no matter what was hatching. There was, then, a lot of leeway as to what a fly was but most fly-fishers could tell you what it wasn't.

I think the problem started, as so many do, in England, with the popularity of reservoir fishing for enormous, often recently planted, semi-tailless stew pond raised rainbows. This brought into the fly-pattern books such monstrosities as Dog Nobblers and Baby Dolls, which could only, I suspect, catch fish because they pissed them off. But soon thereafter came the real change from the traditional, as scarce traditional trout fishing drove fishers after other freshwater species such as bass and onto the oceans for bonefish and other exotic species.

While we had always accepted that a "fly" might include a leech or a freshwater shrimp, now it could imitate a crab, a squid or, perhaps, a bullfrog. It was a short step from this to the use of non-traditional materials such as gold beads, squiggly, ready-made hunks of plastic, or what has now become so fashionable, epoxy. This is a nauseating witches' brew of two sticky globs that must be mixed then moulded into rock hard parts of what we still call a fly. Bits of coloured wood are called a fly because we've attached a feather to them.

No one, I'm sure, would want to make fly-fishing what some people think it is—something akin to a college fraternity or secret lodge where funny raiment and mindless mumbo jumbo determine who's in and who's not. We certainly don't want to go back to the days of poor old G. E. M. Skues, who was driven from the River Test, in Hampshire, for using a nymph, where Halford and his disciples demanded that the then relatively new technique of fishing "dry" be exclusively employed. But surely we must set some minimum standards.

I have such a standard for consideration. A fly must be tied in the traditional sense and with traditional materials. It cannot be manufactured by sticking a hook into a piece of balsa wood and gluing on a feather. And it must—with the exception of the Atlantic Salmon Fly—reasonably represent an aquatic food endemic to the water being fished. Or it might be an attractor in the traditional sense, which is to say, it is constructed from traditional materials, not something retrieved from outer space.

Why exempt Atlantic Salmon Flies from the last rule? Because of tradition. And tradition is all important for it is that which ties us to Haig-Brown, Sparse Grey Hackle, John Waller Hills, Lee Wulff, Frank Sawyer (the inventor of the original Pheasant Tail Nymph), Theodore Gordon and on back to Isaak Walton, Charles Cotton and Dame Julia Berners.

I do not propose that we consider evil anyone who fishes legally with whatever bait or that we even sneer at them even a little bit. I simply propose that we look at our traditions and, after making reasonable allowances for the advances of time, decide who is a fly-fisherman and who is not.

To Hell with Fishing

I stole the title of this essay from Ed Zern, who scripted a wonderful book of the same title that showcased the artwork—we call them, quite wrongly, cartoons—of the great H. T. Webster.

Webster was a marvellous cartoonist with the New York *Tribune*, who created the famous "Caspar Milquetoast" character in the 1920s. H. T. Webster did fishing, hunting and bridge cartoons and they were wonderful. If you can get yourself a copy of the long out-of-print *To Hell with Fishing, or How to Tell Fish from Fishermen* (D. Appleton-Century, 1945) you'll understand why I've named this chapter after it.

What brought on this reminiscence of fly-fishing books I have loved, you ask? Well, in the summer of 2000—the last year of the last millennium for those who can actually count—when Wendy and I moved from a large house in North Vancouver to a small townhouse in the village of Lions Bay, I had to cull 1,500 books from a collection of about 3,000.

This sacrifice involved setting some rules. A first edition of the four volumes of Churchill's *A History of the English Speaking Peoples* (Cassell, 1956–58) was sacrosanct as was a marvellous gold-leafed limited edition of all his newspaper articles. In fact Churchill's books couldn't be touched, period. And other books were off-limits, too. Somehow I had to keep two biographies of Thomas Paine and three of Lord Nelson, other heroes of mine. But right after Churchill and Paine and Nelson came my fly-fishing books—151 of them by actual count. I just couldn't see any I was prepared to part with. None.

Fly-fishing is a sport that, like baseball, has developed a

special and important literature around it. Isaak Walton's *The Compleat Angler* (1653) is, above all else, good, if not great literature. So are writings of dozens of others, including Guy de Maupassant, Ernest Hemingway, Zane Grey and Roderick Haig-Brown, an expatriate Brit who lived the last forty years of his life fishing and writing beautiful prose at Campbell River, British Columbia. Haig-Brown's *A River Never Sleeps* (Lyons, 1946, reprinted 1974) is truly a classic. So is a small book called *Going Fishing* (White Lion Books, 1942) by a very well-known international correspondent, Negley Farson. Farson's book is considered by many to be the best fly-fishing books ever written, along with *Fly Fishing* (Haddon Hall, 1924) by Sir Edward Grey, Viscount of Fallodon, the pre-First World War British Foreign Secretary. They are classic literature in their own right. Ernest Hemingway's son Jack, who died in 2001, wrote a wonderful book entitled *Misadventures of a Fly Fisherman: My Life With and Without Papa* (Taylor Publishing, 1996). Among other things, it tells of him fly-fishing while serving as a commando in occupied France attached to the Resistance, and doing so under the curious and watchful eyes of a German patrol.

G. E. M. Skues, born in Newfoundland but mostly a London solicitor who fished the famous River Test in Hampshire, wrote some wonderful stories, including the classic one "Well, I'm—!", found in many angling anthologies, including Terry Brykczynski, John Thorn and David Reuther's *The Armchair Angler* (Charles Scribner, 1986). The story tells about Mr. Theodore Castwell who, after dying, finds out that what he supposes must be heaven isn't quite what he expected. You'll have to read the story to find out what happens.

Even Rudyard Kipling gets into the act as he tells of the fly-fisherman who, on his back cast, nails a passing cow in "Catching a Cow" in *Fish, Fishing and the Meaning of Life* by Jeremy Paxman (Penguin, 1994). Charles Ritz, the great hotelier, was a lifelong and justly famous angler who wrote some very good stuff, including an autobiography called *A Flyfisher's Life*

(Crown, 1959), which is full of lots of good namedropping times attached to angling with the fly.

One of the funniest stories ever told is John Taintor Foote's *The Wedding Gift and Other Angling Stories* (Lyons, 1924, reprinted 1992). Two very funny stories in this book tell about a New England man of means who, in his forties, marries a much younger woman. His entire life revolves around fly-fishing whereas she couldn't care less about it. They spend their honeymoon together at a faraway camp that features fishing and blackflies, not necessarily in that order. The story of our hero hooking the mighty fish in the home waters and her efforts to follow his instructions to net it is guaranteed to bring loud guffaws from even the most sober of readers. Even funnier, perhaps, is the part when our hero is sent to an auction to get a prize piece of furniture his bride covets and chances upon a bunch of fly-rods under the auctioneer's hammer.

There is, of course Norman MacLean's novella, "A River Runs Through It," published in 1976 in *A River Runs Through It and Other Stories* (University of Chicago Press, 25th Anniversary Edition, 2001), which I think broke the usual rules by being a better movie than a book. But there you are, it's differences of opinion that have you put on one fly while the fish has another insect in mind.

Some interesting people have written very good books about fly-fishing. A New Yorker named Alfred W. Miller, writing under the pseudonym Sparse Grey Hackle, is a delight to read and I'm happy to say that some of his stuff has been reissued recently, including *The Honest Angler: The Best of Sparse Grey Hackle* (Lyons Press, 1998). Chapman Pincher is best known as an expert on spies and a writer of spy stories. Yet he has a couple of very entertaining fly-fishing books, my favourites being *Tight Lines: The Accumulated Lover of a Lifetime's Angling* (Robert Hale, 1997) and *Pastoral Symphony* (Swan Hill Press, 1993).

In recent years, fly-fishing humour has been all but taken over by John Gierach, a trout bum which, incidentally, is the title of one of his books (Gary LaFontaine, 1988). Gierach's humour isn't the roll in the aisles sort of stuff. It's more that you find yourself with a constant grin on your face and a warm feeling in your tummy as he describes the adventures, and often mis-adventures, that you thought happened only to you.

There are other super writers. Ernest Schwiebert, known for his two-volume classic *Trout* (E. P. Dutton, 1978), also spun some super yarns, including *A River for Christmas and Other Stories* (Stephen Greene Press, 1988) and *Death of a Riverkeeper* (Creative Arts Books, 1980). The Englishman, John Waller Hills, will make you believe that you're on his favourite river with *A Summer on the Test* (Philip Allan, 1924) and other won-derful books, including his autobiography called *My Sporting Life* (P. Allan & Co., 1936). I met the late, great fishing corre-spondent for the London *Times*, Conrad Voss Bark—and the author of a couple of dandy books, including *The Encyclopedia of Fly-Fishing* (Batsford, 1986)—at the Arundell Arms in Devon, one of England's premier fishing hotels run by his wife Anne Voss Bark. She is, as she says in her advertisements, "her-self a fly-fisherman." I caught my one and only Atlantic salmon under the guidance of her resident ghillie (guide), David Pilkington. Anne recently was honoured for her lifetime achievement in the fly-fishing world.

There's publisher and writer Nick Lyons, whose fishing mean-derings are accompanied by drawings and water colours by his wife Mari—first class writing and art. There are the marvellous New Zealand writers, my friend John Parsons and his co-author Bryn Hammond as well as O. S. Hintz. And did you know that Arthur Ransome, the famous writer of children's stories, includ-ing the *Swallows* and *Amazon* series, was a great fishing writer? His short story "On Tackle Shops," published in *Rod & Line* (1929, reprinted Flyfisher's Classic Library, 1993) on what a fly-fishing shop should look and smell like—well, it makes you see and smell a fly-fishing shop, that's what it does.

Many more fly-fishing books await. My favourite is a one off.

A retired preacher named David Street wrote a little book called *Fishing in Wild Places* (H.F. & G Witherby, 1990). It's hard as hell to get but a gem when you find it.

Perhaps this interest in fishing literature stems from two things at St. George's School for Boys.

First, I learned very early on that it was best to put your pants back on before flushing the toilet, such was the state of the plumbing. Second, I learned to love literature. We have no plumbing problems at our place in Lions Bay so half my early experience has been wasted. But I do have literature. Every one of my fishing books moved with me. And a hell of a lot of the good literature I have read, a vastly disproportionate amount in fact, is all about the art of angling with the fly.

Thoughts from "Down Under"

Having just returned from my annual trip to New Zealand, my father's homeland, I feel I've just returned from seeing the past. We've all seen the past, you say? But the past I've seen seems so quickly swallowed by the present and the future that it shakes me more than just a bit.

I do my annual fishing in New Zealand on a river that flows into Lake Taupo and is adjacent to the better-known Tongariro, a river Zane Grey made famous when he called New Zealand the "Eldorado" of fishing. My river, the Tauranga-Taupo, is the most beautiful stream that I've ever seen, especially in its higher reaches.

The maps of the Tauranga-Taupo River stop naming pools above the Ranger's Pool simply because no one bothered to fish them in days past. They are spectacularly beautiful. The second pool up from the Ranger's I called the Cathedral Pool many years ago and the name has stuck. The next run up from that I call Rafe's Run because of some spectacular personal victories there (somehow that name hasn't caught on). Nevertheless I do have a little bit of immortality, the Cathedral Pool, on the lovely Tauranga-Taupo. It's not everyone that has successfully named a trout run.

So what's all this in aid of? Well, New Zealand has had some bitter economic pills to swallow in the past twenty-five years and sees that the best permanent source of foreign capital comes, not from its exports, but by importing the hard currency of visitors. And this means big new hotels, and big new hotels mean exploiting touristy things such as rivers full of trout and then pouring anglers, bedecked from head to toe with flashy fishing appurtenances, onto those rivers. I saw my first example a couple of years ago. Wendy and I were fishing a beautiful run in the middle of the Tauranga-Taupo. An American, who bills himself as a tourist guide to avoid becoming a member of the guides association, waded, with his four clients, right into the middle of the stretch Wendy was fishing. These clients, all clad straight from an Orvis catalogue, and the guide himself simply didn't know better. And it will get worse. There is already talk of a big new hotel for the Turangi area, which is right by the mouths of the Tongariro and the Tauranga-Taupo. The Chambers of Commerce are orgasmic at the thought of all those dollars coming in. Those who love the rivers are not.

What were once marvellous, world-class trout streams will now become over-fished semi-sewers where, instead of peace and tranquility, we'll have the New Zealand equivalent of the Vedder River, with wall to wall, argumentative anglers. There will be fights over space, beer cans all over the place and lots and lots of hatchery fish poured into the stream just above the "fishermen." And it will, of course, be seen as progress, especially by those who sell to tourists.

I don't know how you stop "progress" like this. I know that the Tauranga-Taupo wasn't made by God for the near exclusive use of Rafe and Wendy when they pop in once a year. But where does it end?

You can no longer, I'm told, fish the famous New York Beaverkill because of what they call the "aluminum hatch," meaning the masses of canoes, row boats, kayaks and rafts that fill the river any time there's sunshine. People on snowmobiles ruin otherwise remote lakes in the interior of British Columbia through ice fishing.

But don't ice fishermen have the same right to fish as fly-fishers? I suppose they do. But as these rights get exercised and as the merchants get richer, something old fashioned is lost. It's called tranquility. Where once people shared a river with others who wanted gentility and peace, there are now people, smothered with the latest outdoors gadgets, cell phone glued to ear, making sure that they get what they believe they're entitled to.

And they probably are entitled to be noisy boors every bit as much as the person who feels he is entitled to stand in a stream, throw fly line and dream dreams of a civility that will never pass this way again.

RAFE THE KLUTZ

I'm a klutz, a certified klutz. Part of being a klutz is an ongoing self-fulfilling prophecy. When I was a little boy, the more I pasted the cardboard onto my fingers instead of into little tables and chairs, the more the teachers turned me onto tasks more suitable to a kid with ten thumbs. As I got older, it was woodworking classes that exposed my ineptness such that the teacher wouldn't let me near automatic saws and the like. I was restricted to hand saws and making little pocket watch stands for my mother. It was irrelevant that my mother didn't have a pocket watch—nor did my father for that matter. It was a way of keeping Rafe from spilling blood and spoiling everyone's fun.

I entered adulthood without any notion of how to fix things around the house. Either a wife did it, an expensive tradesman came in to do it, or it didn't get done. While I have had a great many wonderful high points in my life, creating something with my hands wasn't one of them.

About thirty-five years ago I moved to Kamloops where, among other things, I was able to indulge my lifetime passion for fishing. I got into fly-fishing in a big way. I used to buy all my stuff, including flies, from the late and much renowned Jack Shaw, who then used to tie flies for Burfields Sports store in Kamloops, alas now long gone. Jack and I became friends and I soaked up his knowledge of the sport we both loved and at which he was an acknowledged expert. (Jack used to drive his poor wife nuts with his aquarium full of aquatic insects. The trouble with aquatic insects is that they eventually hatch and Mrs. Shaw would suddenly be faced with a cloud of mayflies in her living room.)

I would watch Jack tie flies and often make suggestions. Jack would, albeit reluctantly, incorporate my ideas and quite often the fly worked. One day Jack said to me, "Rafe, there's no fishing pleasure like catching a fish on your own personally tied fly. It's been well said that a person may forget the first fish caught but never the first fish he caught on his own tie. I do fly-tying classes, why not come and learn?"

I thought about this and suddenly said, "To hell with it, maybe I'm not as bad a klutz as I think I am. I'm going to have a go." I bought a vise and other rudimentary tools and enrolled in one of Jack's classes.

I did fine for a while. I mastered the tying on a tail, the creation of a chenille body and the making and attaching of a wing. I truly amazed myself and Jack, too.

Then it came time to "whip finish" my fly (tie off the thread at the head). The whip finishing tool is a horrid little bit of twisted metal made all the more horrible by watching people who know how to use it make it look easy. I had met my match. I could not make that damned thing work. I finally flung it across the room, using the same logic I used when tossing a putter after missing a three footer. I gave up on the whole idea of tying flies.

But I brooded. I had been able to make very fundamental flies and I thought that I could master other more complicated ones if only it weren't for that damned whip finisher.

I never liked to admit to fellow anglers that I didn't tie my own flies because everyone whose ability I admired did their own tying. Finally I confessed my inadequacies to a pal over a couple of beers.

"Hell," he said, "I couldn't work that bloody thing either, so I just started tying the fly off with a couple of half hitches by hand and then covered the head with glue. I've never had a fly unravel."

What a revelation! It was like stone tablets on the mountain. I could actually tie flies and not have to go through that unendurable torment. And no one would ever need to know.

I went back to the fly-tying vise and started experimenting. I tied hundreds, perhaps thousands of flies based on the elementary lessons Jack gave me and what I read in "how to" books. Two books were invaluable, both by women—Englishwoman Jacqueline Wakeford's *Flytying* (A. & C. Black, 1983) and the American Helen Shaw's *Fly-Tying* (Lyons Press, 1987).

Early on I decided to recognize my limitations. Some tiers replicate exact imitations of the little critters with all their segments just so. Others in the much broader school, including most of the great fly-tyers, are "impressionists." They try to tie flies that will appeal to the fish, partly because they look like what they are feeding on, but more because they give the impression of a living aquatic insect. Perhaps I should have explained things. Most fly-fishing flies either imitate an aquatic being, give off the impression of being one, or are merely attractors that cause the fish to strike either out of anger or out of curiosity.

Many fly-tiers who are precise imitators waste a great deal of time and effort because they do unnecessary things. For example, it's utterly pointless to worry about what's on top of a fly that floats—a dry fly, which attracts a fish feeding on the surface. The only part of the fly the fish sees is the under body.

I started to tie more and more varieties and, to my surprise and to the surprise of all who watched me paste cardboard to myself in bygone years, I became pretty good. I learned some good lessons along the way that helped. For example, if a particular tie started to go wrong, I learned to start over rather than try to fix things along the way. Moreover, I learned to exercise good quality control: if I didn't like what I'd done, I'd throw it away or, perhaps, give it to a fly-fisherman who I didn't like very much and who didn't recognize rubbish when he saw it.

I achieved great satisfaction from tying my own flies and catching fish on them. I especially enjoyed it when I concocted my own fly-tying pattern and it worked.

Many years ago, while fishing the Tauranga-Taupo, my favourite New Zealand river, with a famous fly called the

Pheasant Tail Nymph I got the idea to tart it up a bit by making the thorax (that's the front part) out of a pearlescent plastic material. It worked like a damn and I gave a couple to my Kiwi friends and excellent fishers Pete and Stella Gordon who pronounced it a great success. I, of course, thought it was my great contribution to the sport of angling and was horrified to see the same pattern presented in a fly-fishing magazine as the invention, many years before, of another angler! With millions of anglers tying flies all over the world, it's unlikely you'll ever tie anything that someone else hasn't already tied.

But in February 2002 I finally did what I had always dreamed of doing—I constructed a fly, from scratch and from my own personal observations and experimentation, that was a huge success. Here's how it happened.

I had been fishing New Zealand rivers in their summer time for many years before I suddenly realized that the damned fish were feeding on the surface even though nothing was hatching in the water. Isn't it strange how often we see something every day without realizing it's there? Sometimes it might be a beautiful bit of scenery you've overlooked, or it may be someone of the opposite sex that you suddenly see for who they are—or it may be a beetle-like creature called the cicada.

In February 2000 Wendy and I began to notice trout taking big slurps from time to time with no obvious candidate for that slurp. I asked our friend Stella Gordon what they were feeding on and she gave me a look of utter amazement. Why cicadas, of course!

Cicadas! Those damned insects make a deafening sound to the point that you sometimes want to shout at them to shut up and yet I'd never stopped to think that they might drop in the river and be delicious morsels.

In fact the process is simple. These large insects are born underground—some of them stay there for years. They hatch when the weather turns hot, moving out of the ground into bushes and trees. There they make a terrible noise by rapidly moving their cellophane-like wings, no doubt for some sexual reason. They are very poor flyers and even worse swimmers so when they get blown into rivers, they became an easy bundle of calories for any neighbouring trout.

I had nothing in my fly box that looked much like a cicada but started throwing at them (with modest success) big flies constructed of deer hair, which helps them float. I started using commercial ties which worked, but they didn't look much like a cicada to me and I assumed that trout were taking them because, being in a hungry mood, they spotted something that piqued their inquisitive nature. While I took some good fish on the dry fly, as did Wendy (who usually out-fishes me by the way), my major accomplishment on this trip was to examine some cicadas in the hope that I could come up with an imitation of my own.

When I got home I went to Ruddick's Fly Shop on Granville Island seeking materials with which to tie the sort of orange and black body the cicada on the Tauranga-Taupo River possess and could find nothing. Then Kathy Ruddick had an idea. They had recently moved their premises from Burnaby and, the new place being smaller, they found it necessary to store a lot of materials. I was welcome to paw through them. I did and found two woolly chenille threads that were perfect to wrap around the hook to simulate the body. I say two chenilles because neither were precisely what I wanted but each in its own way was pretty close.

The obvious characteristic of the cicada in the water is its large wings. I had to find a way to imitate them and again Kathy came to the rescue with a sort of cellophane that, because it was crinkled, looked a lot like the real wing.

Home I went to my vise and to work.

I tied one version with the cellophane wings that to me looked like the real thing. It troubled me, though, because I thought the wing was too obvious. I tried to see the struggling cicada through the eyes of my quarry. It wouldn't see all the wings because the struggling body would partially hide them. So I tied another version and this time, instead of a cellophane wing, I tied some deer hair on top and then on top of that deer hair some narrow strips of silver. What the fish would see would be the body and a solid but subtle impression of a flashing wing.

It was not until the antipodean summer of 2002 that I had a chance to try my luck with my new creations and then only for a day and a half.

The half day came first and I tried the cellophane winged effort. I wasn't at all satisfied. It was hard to cast properly and it tended to land wing down. A couple of small fish took it, though, so it wasn't a failure. But it wasn't exactly a runaway success either.

The next morning Wendy went back to the same stretch of river and she made a rare but serious error. "Why don't you fish this stretch of river with me, honey, and then move to other pools later? I like it when we fish together."

"Why not?" I replied and I knotted on the second variety of cicada, the one with deer hair and silver strips. I had vowed to give this fly a good workout before I rejected it as a failure.

I made a cast near the riffle by the far bank as Wendy was getting herself ready to fish—nothing. Next cast, bang! My heart almost stopped as a five-pound rainbow started jumping up and down through the entire length of the run, ensuring that the fishing would be down for a good half hour after I was through with him. Second cast! And a damned good fish took the fly like he meant it. I landed him with some good-sported help from Wendy who, during the time I was playing the fish, could not herself fish. "Thanks a lot," was the good-natured sarcasm I got as I applied the "priest" to my fish's noggin. (I seldom keep fish but I had promised a couple for friends in Auckland.) I mumbled my half-hearted apologies "for buggering up her pool," kissed my bride goodbye and moved downstream.

To make a long story short, I hooked six other very good fish that day on the second cicada. Bearing in mind that in the summer months two fish a day out of the Tauranga-Taupo river is considered successful, I had to be very satisfied indeed.

Later as I contemplated the day over a beer at the Angler's

Paradise in nearby Turangi, where we were staying, I saw that little boy with paste all over his hands; the little boy who wished he could use the automatic saw, too; the young husband that didn't even own a hammer lest he hurt someone with it; the fly-tying student who couldn't use the contraption that seemed obligatory for the last move. I thought of the thousands of flies I had tied, many quite successful. And I realized that in my own little way I had truly accomplished something. I had observed, pondered, investigated and gone to work. The result was something I had never seen before—something that the highly experienced and effective fly-fishers I talked to in the area had never seen. I had tied a fly that not only looked like a cicada struggling in the water to me and seven good, strong rainbow trout but it was those rainbows that proved me a genius—a very tiny indeed minuscule genius in the great scheme of things but, within my sphere of endeavour, a genius nevertheless.

And that was enough—more than enough. It was the fly-fishing experience of my life.

And that's how a cicada pattern called Wendy's Lament came into being.

ON TRAVEL

THE MAGNETISM OF
LONDON TOWN

I have been to London about eighty times over the past thirty-five years yet I look forward to each visit as though it were my first. Surely, you would think, one must get tired of Buckingham Palace, Madame Tussaud's and the Tower of London. If I visited only tourist haunts, I would be bored, even though Samuel Johnson said, "When a man is tired of London, he is tired of life." But the ways of loving London are all but infinite. Let me, as Elizabeth Barrett Browning did with love, count the ways.

There is the Londoner's intolerance of stupid rules. Only in London do you find the busker playing his saxophone in the Piccadilly Circus tube station right under the sign that reads, "NO BUSKING—FINE 200 POUNDS."

There's the London underground itself. I've had taxi drivers advise me to get out and take the tube because of heavy surface traffic. How could I not "mind," with that voice over the intercom in the underground station telling you to "Mind the gap!"

There's the people watching, especially on a bench in Leicester Square, next to the little statue of Charlie Chaplin.

Then there are the double-decker buses, which give you such a view of the city, as does the Big Bus Company, the best tour of the city.

There are the bookstores, which you can read about in my essay "Book Addiction, The British Version," which follows this one.

There's Hampstead Heath, partly wooded, partly open within Greater London and overlooking it with magnificent views, probably the wonder of the city most overlooked by visitors.

There are the food halls at Harrods. As part of rushing my now wife Wendy, I hustled her down to this great emporium just so she could see the sight of great hanging meats, fresh fish, all imaginable vegetables complete with men and women in overall type aprons. In its way, it rather looked like the old Smithfield's open air food market of decades past. To see this sight of real, fresh food, on the main floor of the world's best department store is something that must be seen to be appreciated.

And there are the Christmas lights, especially on Regent Street but also on Oxford Street, and the Christmas windows, especially in Harrods.

There are the wonderful clothes stores with the superb products of Savile Row, especially the ancient Gieves and Hawkes at No. 1. And there are all the wonderful ladies shops on New Bond Street and Regent Streets. I rate them by the "gentlemen's chairs" they provide. (Louis Feraud is best with Escada and Jaegers close behind.)

There is the superb four park walk that starts at Notting Hill Gate and takes you down Kensington Gardens, across to Hyde Park, under Knightsbridge to Green Park (properly known as The Green Park), across the Mall through St. James's Park to the Parliament Buildings at Parliament Square. (The story as to why Green Park has no flowers goes back to Charles II who, when walking in the park with his Queen, spotted a favourite mistress and plucked a nosegay for her. Queen Catherine was so angry she ordered all the flowers removed from the park.) Right alongside *the* Green Park with the Buckingham Palace grounds on the other side, runs Constitution Hill, which has nothing to do with the British Constitution but was where the same Charles used to "take his constitutional." St. James's Park is where Charles' daddy, one cold January morning, walked to the Banqueting Hall in order to have his head chopped off. It was indeed cold and Charles wore an extra undergarment so that his subjects would not confuse his shivering from cold with shivering from fear. You can visit the Banqueting House (right across from the

Horse Guards Palace on Whitehall) to see where Charles I was beheaded and have a boo at the actual banqueting room and the beautiful murals by Rubens on the ceiling.

In Parliament Square there is the inspiring statue of Churchill, leaning on his cane, jaw jutting as he stares eastward at the approaching Nazi planes, just daring the bastards to take him on.

There's the walk along the South Bank of the Thames with the prospect of the business district of London, dominated by St. Paul's Cathedral, and the used bookstalls, which usually produce at least one "gem" for me.

There's Sung Mattins on Sunday morning at St. Paul's followed by the walk down Ludgate Hill, through Fleet Street and up to Covent Garden. There, in the basement, you can listen to fine live entertainment—a string quartet or opera singers—with a light lunch all for the price of the meal and a pound (if you wish) in the hat. Covent Garden is, of course, where Eliza Doolittle plied her trade as a flower girl until 'enry 'iggins came into her life.

There are the myriad other Sir Christopher Wren churches. St. Martin-within-Ludgate, Wren's smallest church, stands a stone's throw from his masterpiece, St. Paul's. Whereas St. Paul's demonstrates the glory of God, St. Martin's shows the smallness of man. St. Bride's at Ludgate Circus is supposed to have given a baker the idea for the wedding cake and has a wonderful crypt containing Roman ruins. St. Mary-le-Bow's bells mark the true Cockney, who must have been born within their sound to bear proudly that station in life. There's the little café called "The Place Below" at St. Mary-le-Bow. St. Olaves, deep in the financial district on Seething Lane, is where Samuel Pepys and his wife worshipped and are buried. Down the road a bit is All Hallows by-the-Tower from which steeple Pepys watched the Great Fire of 1667. There are the lovely Wren's on the Strand, St. Clement Danes and St. Mary-le-Strand, but have a peek at two rarer ones—the Wren at St. Ann's Soho and the non-Wren at St. Paul's Covent Garden, which is the show biz church and burial ground. Another favourite church, this one by James Gibb (a pupil and sometime partner of Wren's), St. Martin's in the Fields, has wonderful concerts and an ongoing daily flea market.

Here's a rare one for you. Take a look at St. Bartholomew the Great, near the old Smithfield Market. There is a casement over the entrance to the churchyard. After the Great Fire of 1667, Charles II ordered all the fronts of buildings that remained plastered over straight to the ground, eliminating the overhanging balconies that created the wind tunnels that helped the fire to spread. In 1916 a German zeppelin dropped a bomb that exploded outside this casement, causing the plaster to fall away and exposing perfectly preserved Elizabethan architecture, a very rare sight in London. An added treat is the church itself, which some say is the oldest in London.

There are the Thames boat rides to the Thames Barrier, which stops the river from flooding London; to Greenwich (and the zero degree longitude); or to Hampton Court. (If seasickness is, so-to-speak your bag, you can now take the tube, the extended Jubilee line to Greenwich.) And there are the canal rides, especially the Camden Canal.

And there's Jeffrey Archer's penthouse just across the Thames from the Tate Gallery, with wonderful views of the Parliament buildings. I've visited Jeffrey's pad many times—but not for awhile, I fear, as Jeffrey's a long-time guest of Her Majesty now.

There's the revival of the coffee house, so loved by gentlemen of the eighteenth century such as Samuel Johnson, now present in London in the ever-growing form of Starbucks. Not many additions to London are welcomed by me, but this one is. You can now get a bun and a decent cup of coffee at something approaching a reasonable price.

There's the best pizza in town oddly enough in the "400" Café in the basement of Selfridges department store. Selfridges was founded by an American, Gordon Selfridge. Did you know that he married W. Somerset Maugham's former wife after

in the west end, near Selfridges, is also pretty good. If you like postwar jazz, for some reason much more of it, and well re-mastered, is available in the United Kingdom than at home in Canada.

There's the walk along the Victoria Embankment with Cleopatra's needle, which predates Cleo by eons—just why it's called her needle is a bit of a mystery but it has a fascinating history. It was built about 1,500 years before Cleopatra and was brought from Egypt to London in the mid-1800s by a wealthy Englishman. It went down with its ship in a storm in the Bay of Biscay in 1817 and was recovered in 1879. Its twin is on 82nd Street in New York City. Nearby there is a neat little restaurant in the Embankment Gardens for lunch.

There are the pubs, of course—scads of them. I like a midday pint at the Cheshire Cheese, on Fleet Street where Samuel Johnson (whose house is just around the corner) used to hold court. If pubs are your bag—and be prepared to put up with smoke—several guidebooks are obtainable all over London that'll set you on course.

If you're in Knightsbridge, perhaps shopping at Harrods or Harvey Nichols (where Princess Diana had a permanent table in the dining room), then pop over to the Grenadier on Wilmot Place for a pint with a ghost. (It's impossible to find—the pub, that is—which makes it all the more fun.)

Then, I nearly forgot, there is Hyde Park Corner near the Duke of Wellington's home, Apsley House, where Wendy and I often sit under the shadow of the Duke's statue and I pass out advice to lost tourists who, if they're from other parts of Britain, are astonished to be getting directions with a North American accent.

There's a cricket game at the Oval or even better at Lords where you can stroll through the super museum and see relics from the great days of Dr. W. G. Grace, Donald Bradman, Len Hutton or, more recently, Geoffrey Boycott.

There's the bench on New Bond Street with the replicas of Churchill and Roosevelt. There's the short journey down to

Churchill's home at Chartwell, if you're there other than the winter time. You'll be very glad you did. When you go into the sunny dining room overlooking the Weald of Kent it takes little imagination to hear the great man at lunch, telling all the influential what they ought to be doing.

There's the sunny day on a bench in Grosvenor Square where the Canadian Consulate and the American Embassies are located. From there you can stroll through Mayfair, stopping to listen for nightingales in Berkeley Square (you'll not hear any, I'm sad to report). And try for tea at the Ritz (good luck). Mayfair, called by Sidney Smith the "great parallelogram," and named after the annual fair of past years, is a lovely afternoon's walk with Shepherd's Market and friendly pubs.

There is so much more yet—a Sunday stroll through St. James's Park to feed the birds (not the pelicans, though); a visit to the tiny Twinings Tea Shop and museum on the Strand; or a visit to the underground rooms of the War Cabinet on Whitehall, where Churchill often worked and lived during the Second World War.

Yes, friends, there's a lot more to London than the guide books will tell you or you'll see on a tour.

To get to know London a bit, you must, as do I, make it a lifetime commitment.

ORKNEY

I have written and spoken elsewhere about Wendy's and my adventures in Orkney but I'd like to expand on them a bit. There are not many places left in the world where, an hour and a half away by boat from what we know of as "civilization," you can go back in time to quite another era.

For those who don't have an atlas handy, Orkney is an archipelago a few miles north of the Scottish mainland, between it and Shetland, considerably farther to the north. In both cases, incidentally, you must be careful how you name the place— never "the Orkneys" or "the Shetlands" but Orkney or Shetland. "The Shetland Islands" or "the Orkney Islands" are acceptable terms, but in each case the main island is known as "Mainland."

Now, understand, when I say that Orkney is removed from what we know of as civilization, I'm not suggesting that Orcadians don't have the conveniences of life, for they do. I book our bed and breakfast in Stromness by Internet and email and our guide John Grieve keeps in touch with home via cellphone. It's just that the way of life is as it has been for centuries.

They say of Shetlanders that they are fishermen who croft a little while Orcadians are crofters who fish a little. So it remains. Orkney is all farmland and smallish fishing villages. Its two main towns, Kirkwall and Stromness, look as they did in the pictures taken of them in Victorian times.

Tourists are few. The necessary facilities aren't available, for one thing. And Orkney is a long way from where tourists normally roam.

What is it about these barren, almost treeless islands where the wind always blows? Wendy and I have visited there twice in the past two years—I was in Shetland ten years ago—and we are already planning to return. I suppose part of it is the stark beauty. The green is the green of Ireland and the heather, especially in August and September, gives a contrast in colours you don't see anywhere else. The islands are never-ending seascapes, set as they are against the fury of the North Atlantic. The bird-life is extraordinary and the oceans abound in seals and whales.

I suppose, however, that two things mark Orkney as special. First there is the antiquity. There are archaeological digs and a prehistoric village now excavated which goes back perhaps 3,000 years. There are forts, Viking "brochs" and ancient places of worship. And there is the ever-present influence of the Norsemen. In one prehistoric building, Maeshowe, "runic" carvings (Viking graffiti) are scratched on the walls constructed by a civilization that preceded it by 3,000 years!

Second, Orkney's people make the place special. They are not really Scots. As John Grieve put it, "First we're Islanders, second we're Scots and thirdly we're British."

Orkney was under the throne of Norway until 1468 when it came to Scotland because a very broke King Christian of Norway sold the islands to James II of Scotland. Though subsequently populated by some prominent Scots families, notably the Stuarts and the Balfours, the Norse influence remains. These islands are not Gaelic and never have been. The native language, though only sparsely spoken, is Norn, a Norse dialect. Nor is Orkney the place of tartans, kilts and bagpipes. When you're on the islands you feel as if you are with Scots—but only sort of.

Wendy and I have travelled all over the British Isles and Ireland. Enormous differences separate one place from the other. But Orkney is different yet again. The nearest community like theirs is Shetland and Shetland's nearest kin is Norway.

Beautiful, stark, remote, charming, spectacular, mostly, Orkney is different, very different.

Book Addiction:
The British Version

Everyone displays addictive behaviour of some sort. I have no drug addictions—save perhaps a beer or two at timely moments—but I certainly have three of another variety—Wendy, London and bookstores. When they combine, the opiate is irresistible.

London has, of course, very good new bookstores and Wendy loves to prowl them as much as I do. The huge Waterstone's on Piccadilly has taken over the five floors of the old Robert Simpson department store. Still on Piccadilly, Hatchards sensibly has a special "Churchill" section with used books on the great man. On Charing Cross Road are the old bookstores, the remainder stores and what is still billed the "World's Biggest," Foyles. The small but superb Bookthrift in Thurloe Place in South Kensington—they have other branches outside London—carries brand new books, the ones you want, at a substantial discount, plus the books you paid twenty-five quid for last year now at half the price.

Where Wendy and I literally part company for a few hours when in London is at the Leicester Square tube station. There, a few yards away, the Charing Cross Road used bookstores abound. Several new bookstores can be found there as well.

Wendy's tastes in books run to what I would call—and she would deny—the occult. She's a mystic and loves books about mystical experiences. She also has a penchant to read women's books, health books (especially non-traditional) and novels of all sorts. Her tastes are more catholic than mine and she tends to look for what's new. I, on the other hand, have rather restricted tastes, running to biographies, histories, politics and good fly-fishing writing.

We have a deal, my Wendy and I. For two or three hours each trip we part company so she can do things she especially likes to do and which bore me, and I can canvass Charing Cross Road and immerse myself in the used bookstores thereon.

Used bookstores have much in common with good fishing tackle shops. Both have a distinctive odour. It is an odour that rouses the browsing passion immediately. They have a sort of dishevelled look of madness about them and an atmosphere guaranteed to make you buy what you didn't know you wanted until it confronted you. Both emporia also have proprietors who somehow know where everything is located in their disorganized, uncatalogued shop.

Proprietors of fly-fishing shops and used bookstores are excellent buyers. There are no bargains—at least I've yet to find them. That's not to say that there aren't good buys, just that the rare first edition of Isaak Walton's *The Compleat Angler* (1653), for five pounds is never to be found and never will be even in stores owned by people who don't fish.

Some years ago a British fly-fishing magazine did a poll which decided that the best book ever written about fly-fishing was called *Going Fishing* (White Lion Books, 1942) by an American foreign correspondent named Negley Farson. One day shortly thereafter, I was in a used bookstore on Charing Cross Road when I chanced upon a very fine copy of this book—first edition, complete with dust jacket, for twenty pounds. What a bargain! I shivered with excitement when paying for it, sure that the proprietor, seeing my excitement, would realize that he was parting with a priceless book at a ridiculous price. Like a dog who pinches a bone from the butcher, I scampered out the door feeling a little ashamed of myself for having taken such advantage of the poor chap who was obviously barely eking out a living.

I later found, through catalogues and seeing other copies of this book, that rather than cheating the bookseller, I actually paid a couple of quid too much! Negley Farson may have written the best fly-fishing book of all time but they're a dime a dozen in the used book trade. Hope springs eternal, however, that one will plough through stacks of books and come up with a priceless first edition that the seller has in his bin of one pound each.

The first used bookstore you'll find as you walk up Charing Cross Road is Quinto Books at No. 48. This is an excellent two-floored store, where you will find lots of good stuff on all topics. Next door is The Charing Cross Book Store, which, it would seem, is in some sort of partnership with its neighbour, Henry Pordes Books. The two shops are excellent places to browse for a very long time. If you browse as I do, each could easily use up several hours.

On my last trip to Britain I was saddened to learn that Any Amount of Books at No. 62 Charing Cross Road (where I bought the Farson book) was closing and that I had missed the best of a sale by a few days. The store will, I suppose, now become a mobile phone emporium and thus do a double job of depriving us of a small but nevertheless important part of our culture and further harming what's left of our civilization.

Moving north up Charing Cross brings you to The Silver Moon Women's Bookshop which, I gather from the window display, equally sources books for lesbians and those of the female persuasion who do not yet believe that they own and control the world lock, stock and barrel.

The next three shops on Charing Cross are devoted to specialties—design, mid-eastern and Muslim studies, and the media. Even if these subjects don't interest you, they're worth a boo.

Thus ends the used book row. I have not mentioned antiquarian bookshops because they are outside my addiction. A couple of "remainder" stores farther up the block often have books in them at maddeningly low prices when you consider what you paid for them off the press.

I can't leave Charing Cross Road without mentioning again what bills itself as the World's Largest Bookstore—the famous

Foyles. I was very disappointed in Foyles at my last visit for it has actually become reasonably efficient and up-to-date—forced to become so, no doubt, by the marketing skills of Waterstone's, which has branches all over London. (On my last visit to London I saw that Waterstone's on Charing Cross Road across the road from Foyles had packed it in.)

When I first started shopping at Foyles, thirty-five years ago, it was a delight. Everything was all over everywhere and you simply were forced to explore its five floors. They were connected by a lift which, if it wasn't the inventor's first, was damned near. I well remember finding the Winston Churchill section in the midst of the "Technical Section" and somehow it didn't surprise me. Moreover, Foyles took no credit cards and, when it came to finding things, the staff had no more clue than you did. One did not drop into Foyles, one allotted it at least a full morning. Now the elevator has been replaced by shiny new escalators, the books are in a reasonable semblance of order, credit cards are welcome and the staff knowledgeable. It is indeed quite a comedown and marks the end of an era when, because organization was all but missing, you really had to be an experienced and competent book prowler to find what you were looking for.

Overall, Britain is chock-a-block with used bookstores. A year or two ago I scrambled through the open air book market on the south bank of the Thames and found a mint copy of *Alice in Wonderland*—with the original Tenniel illustrations, not Walt Disney's cruddy version—for eight pounds and bought it for my youngest grandchild, Karyn Leigh. Her mom, who had never read the book—that says something rather unflattering about her upbringing—didn't care for it much but Karyn Leigh just loved it.

Every village in Britain of any consequence has at least one used bookstore. There's a damned good one in Kirkwall in Orkney, for example. The beauty is that you can find British books you always wanted and which are not available at home. In fact the small town of Wigtown in Scotland boasts more than a dozen used bookeries, some of them being very specialized. And one must mention Hay-on-Wye, through which the England–Wales border passes, which is considered (and considers itself) the used book capital of the world.

A code of conduct is involved in buying used books. Because everything is so crowded, it would help if you could somehow be a combination of Michael Jordan and Toulouse-Lautrec with a rubber neck. Great patience is required when sharing narrow corridors with other browsers. And you must whisper. Why, I don't know, but you just must.

Some owners will bargain but I have found that the mere suggestion of a deal is usually met with a stern look down the nose. It's as if you asked a priest if you could borrow a buck or two from the poor box.

Finally, I must tell you that there is another similarity between my favourite stores, the fly-fishing shop and the used bookstore. They take a bit of getting used to. The massive array of things for sale can be quite formidable until you accustom yourself to how they are usually laid out, where things can be found and how to value what you see.

Taken as a whole, buying books, while an expensive addiction, is really a very neat way to spend some time—especially in Britain.